To [illegible],

One of the more creative souls I know. I think you'll enjoy this.

Love,

Mark

THE CREATIVE SPIRIT

DANIEL GOLEMAN

PAUL KAUFMAN

MICHAEL RAY

A DUTTON BOOK

**To Maxwell and Julia Kaufman, who made it possible
for so many others to live creative lives.**

DUTTON
Published by the Penguin Group
Penguin Books USA Inc., 375 Hudson Street, New York, New York, 10014, U.S.A.
Penguin Books Ltd., 27 Wrights Lane, London, W8 5TZ, England
Penguin Books Australia Ltd, Ringwood, Victoria, Australia
Penguin Books Canada Ltd, 10 Alcorn Avenue, Toronto, Ontario, Canada M4V 3B2
Penguin Books (N.Z.) Ltd, 182–290 Wairau Road, Auckland 10, New Zealand

Penguin Books Ltd, Registered Offices: Harmondsworth, Middlesex, England

First published by Dutton, an imprint of New American Library, a division of Penguin Books USA Inc.
Distributed in Canada by McClelland & Stewart Inc.

First Printing March, 1992
10 9 8 7 6 5 4 3 2

Copyright © Alvin H. Perlmutter, Inc., 1992
All rights reserved.
"The Creative Spirit" television series, a production of Alvin H. Perlmutter, Inc.,
is presented by WETA, Washington, D.C., for broadcast on PBS and funded by IBM.

Please see page 176 for permissions, animation credits, and photo credits that do not appear in the text.

Dutton logo REGISTERED TRADEMARK—MARCA REGISTRADA

LIBRARY OF CONGRESS CATALOGING-IN-PUBLICATION DATA:

Goleman, Daniel.
The creative spirit / Daniel Goleman, Paul Kaufman, and Michael Ray.
p. cm.
"The Creative Spirit television series, a production of Alvin H. Perlmutter, Inc. is presented by WETA,
Washington D.C., for broadcast on PBS."
ISBN 0-525-93354-9
1. Creative ability. I. Kaufman, Paul. 1935-   . II. Ray, Michael L. III. Title.

BF408.G57 1992
153.3'5—dc20   91-36411

Printed in the United States of America
Set in Adobe Minion
Designed by Impress

Acknowledgments

S THIS BOOK is inspired by interviews with participants in "The Creative Spirit" television series, you will find the names of the people who helped produce the television programs on page 177. We thank them all. We are especially grateful to Lisa Sonne, whose research helped define the intellectual scope of the television series and who became one of its producers. In particular, we thank those on the production staff who helped determine the content of the series through story development and producing: Catherine Tatge, Sunde Smith, Anne-Marie Cunniffe, Anne Hansen, and John Andrews. Animators Chuck Jones and John Canemaker generously contributed their artistry and wit to both the series and the book.

The organization and management of the entire *Creative Spirit* project benefited from the experience and insight of Executive Producer Alvin H. Perlmutter. The collaboration of IBM was essential to giving the series and book their international scope and flavor. We are very grateful for the enthusiastic support of Arlene Wendt, Bill Harrison, Cal LaRoche, and Michael Gury.

We deeply appreciate the contributions of Howard Gardner, Teresa Amabile, Mike Csikszentmihalyi, Kenneth Kraft, Benny Golson, Jim Collins, James Parks Morton, Dori Shallcross, Hisashi Imai, Loris Malaguzzi, Tiziana Filipini, Jan Carlzon, Anita Roddick, Rolf Osterberg, Herman Maynard, Wayne Silby, Sheridan Tatsuno, Dee Dickinson, Tara Bennett Goleman, Jennifer and Karen Kaufman, Kathleen Speeth, and Kenneth Dychtwald.

We are indebted to Linda and Valerie Jones for giving us temporary loan of that Sisyphus of the sagebrush, Mr. Great Ideas himself: Wile E. Coyote.

For their inspired and patient collaboration in the design and production of this book, we thank Hans Teensma, Ginger Barr Heafey, Al Crane, and Jeff Potter.

Finally, we thank our editor, Rachel Klayman, whose creativity and care were absolutely essential to the writing and production of this book.

CONTENTS

Preface

✦◉✦
WILE E. COYOTE
MEETS THE BUDDHA

HUCK JONES, the animator who fathered Wile E. Coyote (one of the stars of the television series on which this book is based), says that in order to draw a coyote "you have to have a coyote inside of you. And you have to get it out. Animation means to invoke life and how do you invoke life? *You have to find it within yourself.*"

When we were producing *The Creative Spirit* television series on location in Kyoto, Japan, a carver of Buddhist figures told us: "When I carve, I look for the Buddha *in the wood.* And, when I am carving, I need to bring the Buddha out of the wood. I have to be very careful not to cut the Buddha." Between Mr. Coyote and the Buddha lurks a truth. For creativity to happen, something within us must be brought to life in something outside of us.

In producing the series, we asked many different kinds of people around the world how they go about finding and using their creativity. We interviewed workers at a heavy machinery factory in Sweden where all of the employees have the same job description: "Responsible Person." Each worker personally signs the piece he manufactures. "The products we make," says the company's founder, "are expressions of who we are."

We saw Italian schoolchildren create extraordinarily original paintings which blazed with pure color and fantastical shapes. *Niente senza gioia* —"nothing without joy"—was the school's motto. In Iowa, we watched managers for a utility company put themselves through the rigors of a "ropes course" in order to overcome the fear of taking risks and to learn to trust others. Joy, responsibility, trust...this was the universal language of the creative spirit.

As to our inventive friend, Wile E. Coyote, what would happen if he actually met the Buddha on a road in the desert? Would he strike up a philosophical conversation about the futility of chasing Road Runners or why he continues to buy products from Acme that never work? Or perhaps he would recall the saying: "If you meet the Buddha on the road, kill him." The idea is that this Buddha is merely an illusion of enlightenment, and you must first look within yourself for what you seek. Anyone in dogged pursuit of creativity might interpret that bit of sage advice to mean: if you're looking to find the creative spirit somewhere outside of yourself, you're looking in the wrong place.

The "spirit" in the title of this book means the breath of life, and the Swedish worker reveals his spirit in the piece of steel he shapes and polishes. And the creative spirit is *within you*—whatever you do. The catch, of course, is to liberate it. We hope this book will help.

PAUL KAUFMAN
Senior Producer and Writer
The Creative Spirit Television Series

CHAPTER ONE

INSIDE CREATIVITY

In every work of genius we recognize our own rejected thoughts.

—Ralph Waldo Emerson

HAS THIS ever happened to you?

You're out for a jog, you're completely relaxed, your mind a pleasant blank.

Then all of a sudden into your head pops the solution to a problem you've been mulling over for days or weeks. You can't help but wonder why you didn't think of it before....

In such moments you've made contact with the creative spirit, that elusive muse of good—and sometimes great—ideas. The creative spirit is more than an occasional insight or whimsical flourish. When the creative spirit stirs, it animates a style of being: a lifetime filled with the desire to innovate, to explore new ways of doing things, to bring dreams to reality.

No matter who you are, the creative spirit can enter your life. It is at hand for anyone who has the urge to tinker, to explore new possibilities, to leave things a little better than before. The creative spirit was at work, for example, in the life of Martin Luther King, Jr., whose vision and nonviolent social tactics changed his nation. And it was at work throughout the life of Martha Graham, who continued to transform modern dance up to her death at ninety-six. But that spirit also shows up in the adventurous cook who continually invents recipes, or the inspiring teacher who constantly finds new ways to challenge students.

Creative moments are vital to everything we do in any area of life: relationships, family, work, community. In this chapter we're going to examine the anatomy of the creative moment and explore the essence of creativity.

When you take a new approach to what you're doing—and the new approach works—you're using your creativity. When you go beyond the traditional ways of solving a problem with a success that influences others, your creativity takes on a vital social dimension.

In this chapter we'll meet people who embody the passion, persistence, and humor that bring the creative spirit to life, including:

● **Jim Collins,** whose teaching at Stanford's Graduate School of Business is informed by the lessons he learns as a risk-taking, world-class rock climber.

● **Dr. Alexa Canady,** a pediatric neurosurgeon who has found creative ways of listening to, and learning from, her patients.

● **Paul MacCready,** the prolific inventor who built the Gossamer Condor—the world's first successful human-powered plane—by questioning some basic assumptions of aircraft design.

● And **Chuck Jones,** the legendary animator of Bugs Bunny, Wile E. Coyote, and Daffy Duck, who believes that fearing the "dragon" of anxiety is the necessary springboard to creativity.

And in the pages of this book, we'll look at what parents can do to help a child discover early interests that can grow into a lifetime of enthusiasm, and avoid the "creativity killers" that stifle a child's fertile imagination. We'll journey to Italy to visit one of the world's finest preschools and to an Indianapolis elementary school designed to expose children to a range of creative projects far beyond the usual narrow band of school subjects. And we'll see how a children's Olympics for creativity challenges and motivates its contestants with healthy competition.

Next, we'll visit pioneering companies around the world that have

found fascinating ways of enhancing the creativity of their workers. A Swedish company does away with restrictive job titles, hierarchical management, and financial secrets. Their goal: to put the ultimate responsibility for innovation and problem-solving into the hands of all the workers. A California firm provides child care on the premises and a more homelike environment to reduce stress. The theory: workers who can see their children at any time will worry less and be happier—more giving on the job. An Iowa company takes its workers to the countryside to go through an obstacle course so that back at the office they learn to trust each other and to take creative risks.

Then we'll see ways in which people the world over are using their creative spirit to find innovative responses to pressing human needs. In a search for creative altruism, we'll meet a group of Hispanic women in Texas who have banded together to raise their families. A high-tech Japanese company uses innovative robotics so that people with severe handicaps can work. Swedish children hold country fairs and write songs to raise money to save a rain forest in Costa Rica. To battle poverty and hopelessness, an inner-city church trains members of the community to become skilled stone masons.

Finally, we will consider how our society might engineer a widespread Renaissance of creativity. We'll visit the Arizona desert to explore the challenging thesis that the secret to our creative rebirth can be found within Nature herself.

And throughout these pages run suggestions on how to let the creative spirit infuse your life—including exercises to help still that dreaded inner voice of self-judgment and to help awaken your wonder and intuition.

Anatomy of the Creative Moment

✴❀✴ PAVING THE WAY

ACK TO our jogger.

That flash of inspiration, that instant when you solve a problem you've grappled with for weeks, is the final moment of a process marked by distinctive stages. The nineteenth-century French mathematician Henri Poincaré—who realized in a flash the solution to a difficult mathematical problem while mulling it over on vacation—was among the first to propose what are still regarded as the basic steps in creative problem-solving.

The first stage is preparation, when you immerse yourself in the problem, searching out any information that might be relevant. It's when you let your imagination roam free, open yourself to anything that is even vaguely relevant to the problem. The idea is to gather a broad range of data so that unusual and unlikely elements can begin to juxtapose themselves. Being receptive, being able to listen openly and well, is a crucial skill here.

That's easier said than done. We are used to our mundane way of thinking about solutions. Psychologists call the trap of the routine "functional fixedness": we see only the obvious way of looking at a problem—the same comfortable way we always think about it. The result is sometimes jokingly called "psychosclerosis"—hardening of the attitudes.

Another barrier to taking in fresh information is self-censorship, that inner voice of judgment that confines our creative spirit within the boundaries of what we deem acceptable. It's the voice of judgment that whispers to you, "They'll think I'm foolish," "That will never work," or "That's too obvious."

> *"You have to be with the work and the work has to be with you. It absorbs you totally, and you absorb it totally."*
> —LOUISE NEVELSON, SCULPTRESS

We can learn to recognize this voice of judgment, and have the courage to discount its destructive advice. Remind yourself of what Mark Twain once said: "The man with a new idea is a crank until the idea succeeds."

To the stage of preparation we can add another, which, because it's very uncomfortable, is often overlooked: frustration. Frustration arises at the point when the rational, analytic mind, searching laboriously for a solution, reaches the limit of its abilities. Says Stanford's Jim Collins, who teaches creativity to some of the world's best young businesspeople, "If you talk to people who have done really creative things, they'll tell you about the long hours, the anguish, the frustration, all the preparation before something clicks and bam! you move forward with a great leap. But they can't make a great leap without working their brains out."

Although no one enjoys frustration and despair, people who sustain their creativity over the course of a lifetime do come to accept periods of anguish as necessary parts of the whole creative process. Accepting that there is an inevitable "darkness before the dawn" helps in several ways. When the darkness is seen as a necessary prelude to the creative light, one is less likely to ascribe frustration to personal inadequacy or label it "bad." This more positive view of anxiety can foster a greater willingness to persist in trying to solve a problem, in spite of the frustration. Since evidence suggests that people often fail to solve problems not because the problems are insoluble but because they give up prematurely, persistence can be seen as one of our greatest allies. However, there often comes a point when the wisest course of action is to cease all effort. At this moment, the rational mind "surrenders" to the problem.

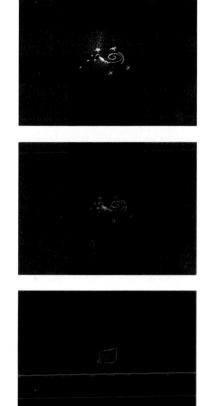

The creative spirit meets the voice of judgment.

INCUBATION

ONCE YOU HAVE mulled over all the relevant pieces and pushed your rational mind to the limits, you can let the problem simmer. This is the incubation stage, when you digest all you have gathered. Whereas preparation demands active work, incubation is more passive, a stage when much of what goes on occurs outside your focused awareness, in the mind's

STEPS INTO THE DARKNESS

Creative people are committed to risk," says Benny Golson, jazz musician and composer. "The creative person always walks two steps into the darkness. Everybody can see what's in the light. They can imitate it, they can underscore it, they can modify it, they can reshape it. But the real heroes delve in darkness of the unknown.

"It's where you discover 'other things.' I say other things because when the new things are discovered, they have no name and they sometimes defy description—like a newborn baby. He has no name, he defies description. He's wrinkled. He looks like his grandfather but he's only one day old. He looks like his mother, but he also looks like his father. But after a while he's beautiful and he's got a name. And many times that's the way our ideas are, the ones we create from darkness. Darkness is important—and the risk that goes along with it."

unconscious. As the saying goes, you "sleep on it."

Although you may pluck the problem from this mental twilight zone from time to time and devote your full attention to it, your mind continues to seek a solution whether or not you are consciously thinking about the problem. Indeed, the answer may come to you in a dream, or in that dreamlike state as you are on the verge of sleep, or on first awakening in the morning.

We often underestimate the power of the unconscious mind. But it is far more suited to a creative insight than is the conscious mind. There are no self-censoring judgments in the unconscious, where ideas are free to recombine with other ideas in novel patterns and unpredictable associations in a kind of promiscuous fluidity.

Another strength of the unconscious mind is that it is the storehouse of everything you know, including things you can't readily call into awareness. Cognitive scientists, who study how information flows through the brain, tell us that all memory is unconscious before it becomes conscious, and that only a very small fraction of what the mind takes in—less than one percent—ever reaches conscious awareness. In this sense, the unconscious mind is intellectually richer than the conscious part of the mind: it has more data from which to draw upon.

Further, the unconscious speaks to us in ways that go beyond words. What the unconscious mind knows includes the deep feelings and rich imagery that constitutes the intelligence of the senses. What the unconscious mind knows is often more apparent as a felt sense of correctness— a hunch. We call this kind of knowing intuition.

Our intuition draws directly on the vast storehouse of information which is an open book to the unconscious, but to some degree closed to consciousness. That is why, for instance, courses preparing students to take the Scholastic Aptitude Test advise that if we are stumped by a question, we should make as our guess the first answer that seems right. Indeed, experimental studies have found that people's first hunches generally form the basis for better decisions than those decisions made after rationally working through the pros and cons. When we trust our intuition, we are really turning to the wisdom of the unconscious.

PERCHANCE TO DAYDREAM

WE ARE MORE open to insights from the unconscious mind in moments of reverie, when we are not thinking of anything in particular. That is why daydreams are so useful in the quest for creativity. The fruitfulness of first immersing yourself in a problem, then setting it aside for a while, jibes with the experience of Paul MacCready, an inventor who has tackled creative challenges such as building a human-powered airplane. "You have to get yourself immersed in the subject, and to a certain extent you need some good technical preparation in order to get started," says MacCready. "Then, if it gets interesting to you, you start thinking about it at odd hours. Maybe you can't come up with a solution, and you forget about it for a while, and suddenly while you're shaving you get a good idea."

Shaving is one of MacCready's most creative times: "You have to concentrate just enough so there aren't too many distractions, and you often find yourself thinking of wildly different subjects and coming up with solutions to some of the day's challenges or some of the big projects you are dealing with."

Anytime you can just daydream and relax is useful in the creative process: a shower, long drives, a quiet walk. For example, Nolan Bushnell, the founder of the Atari company, got the inspiration for what became a best-selling video game while idly flicking sand on a beach.

Some people get their best ideas in the shower.

"The only big ideas I've ever had have come from daydreaming, but modern life seems intent on keeping people from daydreaming," Paul MacCready adds. "Every moment of the day your mind is being occupied, controlled, by someone else. At school, at work, watching television—it's somebody else's mind controlling what you think about. Getting away from all that is really important. You need to kick back in a chair or get in a car without having the radio on—and just let your mind daydream."

Wayne Silby, a founder of the Calvert Group, one of the first and largest socially responsible investment funds, took a more deliberate approach to harnessing his unconscious. A change in banking laws was about to make obsolete the main investment tool the fund had used. While funds like Calvert had always been able to offer money market accounts at a higher interest rate than any banks could offer, suddenly banks, too, could offer the same investment. The main competitive advantage for Calvert—and all similar investment funds—was about to vanish.

So Silby went into a sensory deprivation tank—in which all sounds, sights, and other stimuli are muted—to meditate on the problem. "You need to have a space where your mental chatter and all the judgments and loudspeakers in your mind about who you are and what you are doing are turned down. And then you can get in touch with a deeper part of yourself that can start revealing patterns."

In the isolation tank Silby came up with a solution: a new financial instrument that allowed Calvert to cooperate, rather than compete, with the banks. The instrument, in short, let Calvert funnel its investors' money into the dozen or so banks with the highest interest rates. The customers got the best return on their funds, while the banks gave Calvert an extra fee. The result: maintaining close to a billion dollars in business.

ILLUMINATION

WITH LUCK, immersion and daydreaming lead to illumination, when all of a sudden the answer comes to you as if from nowhere. This is the stage that usually gets all the glory and attention. This is the moment that people sweat and long for, the feeling "This is it!"

But the thought alone—even if it is a breakthrough realization—is still not a creative act. The final stage is translation, when you take your insight and transform it into action. Translating your illumination into

All the really good ideas I ever had came to me while I was milking a cow.
—GRANT WOOD, PAINTER

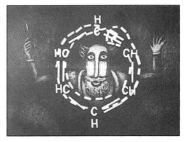

Well, the creative spirit has struck again, this time on a cool evening in 1865. The chemist Friedrich Kekulé has just discovered the elusive structure of the benzene molecule, a major breakthrough in organic chemistry. Kekulé credits his breakthrough—and we'll have to take his word on this—to a daydream.

Mr. Kekulé reports that after a long day of thinking, he was relaxing in front of a fire, just watching embers fly up in circular patterns. He says he then became transfixed and fell into a reverie, and as he half-dozed, he began to see the sparks dance in a snakelike way. Suddenly, the sparks formed a whirling circle as if it were a snake biting its own tail. Kekulé says he then awoke in a flash with a now, accurate picture of the structure of a benzene molecule: a ring!

Kekulé's approach to problem-solving: do a lot of hard thinking, then relax and let yourself dream.

reality makes your great idea more than just a passing thought; it becomes useful to you and to others.

Any model of the stages in the creative process is only a rough approximation of a process that is actually quite fluid and can follow any number of courses. A writer or artist may have an ongoing series of illuminations that carry him through the entire work, from beginning to end. Or an inventor may find that most of her working time is spent in preparation and execution—the ninety-nine percent of genius that, as Edison told us, is perspiration, not inspiration.

More often over the course of a complex creation, like writing a screenplay or designing a building, the act of creation is a long series of acts, with multiple and cascading preparations, frustrations, incubations, illuminations, and translations into action.

Grand Visions and Tiny Closets

OUR LIVES CAN be filled with creative moments, whatever we do, as long as we're flexible and open to new possibilities—willing to push beyond the routine. Consider the myriad faces of creativity:

* Groundbreaking ideas, like debt-for-land swaps that save tropical forests while helping impoverished countries, or the theory of relativity, or the concept of genetic engineering

* The imaginative expression of caring and compassion: "meals-on-wheels" that bring food to the homebound, birthing rooms, the AIDS Quilt, Gandhi's strategy of protesting injustice with nonviolence

* Grand visions of hope and truth that show the way to others—the Bill of Rights and the Gettysburg Address, Martin Luther King's "I have a dream" speech

* Bright ideas that get you out of a logjam, like figuring out how to squeeze three more feet of closet space out of your bedroom, or how to pack more time into your day to exercise, without giving up any of the other things you have to—or love to—do.

Whether great or small, each of these examples points to the essence of a creative act: one that is both novel and appropriate. An innovation is different from what's been done before—but that's not enough: it can't be just bizarre or eccentric. It must "work." To be creative, it must somehow be correct, useful, valuable, meaningful.

The everyday expression of creativity often takes the form of trying out a new approach to a familiar dilemma. Says Dr. Teresa Amabile, a psychologist at Brandeis University whose research is on creativity: "At work, a manager dealing with a sticky relationship between two workers can show creativity in how she handles it. She can get them to talk things over from a new perspective, or maybe bring in a third person to work with the other two, or figure out a practical way of separating them physically. It's not on the order of creativity that wins a Nobel Prize, but it is novel and it works."

CREATIVITY IS AKIN
TO LEADERSHIP

HOWEVER, it's not enough just to be novel and useful: an important dimension of creativity—especially the kinds of efforts that influence others and for which people become famous—is the audience. There is a crucial social dimension to the creative act.

"Being creative means you do something which is first of all unusual," says Howard Gardner, a developmental psychologist at Harvard University. "But it also makes enough sense, even though it's unusual, that other people take it seriously. I mean, I could talk while standing on my head, and that would be unusual, but unless I and other people found it was somehow adaptive, I couldn't be called creative for it.

"But if, say, I'd found some way to convey twice as much information in the same period of time and make you enjoy it more, that would be creative. And even if it were very unusual, it would catch on because it's an effective thing to do."

In short, how a creative effort is received makes a difference. Yet it can be argued that much of the world's creativity takes place anonymously in private moments, just for the pure pleasure of it, or for the joy of using one's talents in effective or beautiful ways. A flower arrangement in the living room, a poem in a private journal, or a cleverly constructed model boat may express creativity and never have an audience beyond the maker.

Some people get their best ideas while driving.

But for every act of creativity meant to have a larger impact, there needs to be an appropriate audience. In high-energy physics that audience consists of a few dozen scientific peers; in painting it might be a loose network of gallery owners, critics, and art lovers. The opinions of these audi-

A Program to Strengthen Your Creativity

The French playwright Molière tells the story of a countryman who asked what prose was, and was astonished to find that he had been speaking it all his life. It's the same with creativity, which half the world thinks of as a mysterious quality that the other half possesses. A good deal of research suggests, however, that everyone is capable of tapping into his or her creative spirit. This section, which continues throughout the book, presents a modest program you can use in your own way, at your own speed, to become more creative at what you do. We don't mean just getting better ideas. We're talking about a kind of general awareness that leads to greater enjoyment of your work and the people in your life: a spirit that can improve collaboration and communication with others.

The exercises and guidelines ahead are based on one simple principle: your creativity increases as you become more aware of your own creative acts. The more you can experience your own originality, the more confidence you get, the greater the probability that you'll be creative in the future. These

ences count far more in evaluating creativity than do the views of millions of others who have no expertise in the relevant field. Of course, that does not mean that critics are the final arbiter of a creative act. "Sophisticated" critics of the day, for instance, panned many of the greatest painters, including Monet and Van Gogh.

Indeed, many of the world's most creative people have had to spend years pursuing their craft in a lonely vigil, hounded by naysayers. Virtually none of the great men and women whose creative drive has transformed the discipline in which they worked was met with acceptance at first. Most were attacked, but knew in their hearts that theirs was the right course anyway.

Creative efforts that do take hold in a given field must be persuasive to others. In the view of Professor Dean Simonton, this social dimension makes creativity akin to leadership: "A successful leader is someone who can persuade people to change their ideas or behavior. A successful creator is someone who gives other people a different way of looking at the world.

"It may be a different way of feeling about the world if it's creativity in the arts, like in poetry or painting, or a different way of understanding the world if it's in the sciences," Simonton adds. "But in any case creativity is not something that's entirely within the individual—it involves reaching other people. It's a social fact, not just a psychological one. Creativity is not something that a person keeps in the closet; it comes into existence during the process of interacting with others."

◉ BEING CREATIVE IN X

The social setting for creativity is usually one's field or domain. Says Howard Gardner, "A person isn't creative in general—you can't just say a person is 'creative.' You have to say he or she is creative in X, whether it's writing, being a teacher, or running an organization. People are creative in something."

Creativity is not a single ability that can be used by a person in any activity. According to Gardner, "Creativity isn't some kind of fluid that can ooze in any direction. The life of the mind is divided into different regions, which I call 'intelligences,' like math, language, or music. And a given person can be very original and inventive, even iconoclastically imaginative, in one of those areas without being particularly creative in any of the others."

This leads Gardner to view the creative individual as "someone who can regularly solve a problem, or can come up with something novel that becomes a valued product in a given domain." Gardner's definition of creativity is a departure from the ones found in most psychology textbooks. In those books creativity is described as some kind of global talent. Along with this view is the popular notion of handy tests that can tell people in a few minutes how creative they are.

The textbook view of creativity, says Gardner, "doesn't make any sense at all. I think you have to watch a person working for a while in a particular domain, whether it's chess, piano-playing, architecture, or trying to start a business or run a meeting. And you have to see what they do when problems come up, and how their solution is received. Then you can make your judgments about whether that person is creative or not.

"Now, the creative person," Gardner says, "has to be able to do that sort of thing regularly. It's not a flash-in-the-pan, one-time-only thing. It's a whole style of existence. People who are creative are always thinking about the domains in which they work. They're always tinkering. They're always saying, 'What makes sense here, what doesn't make sense?' And if it doesn't make sense, 'Can I do something about it?' "

exercises have been developed in classes on creativity at Stanford University. Over the past thirteen years, thousands of people from all walks of life, from all over the world, have practiced them.

One thing that we've learned is that creativity is not just a mental game. The relationships between thinking and feelings, between mind and body, are critical to unleashing creativity.

Tensions that constrict the flow of ideas through the mind are analogous to tensions that constrict the flow of blood through the muscles of the body. Our experience has been that the simple act of physical relaxation—letting go—frees the mind to be open to new ideas. The goal of many of the exercises in this program is to encourage thinking of the mind and body as a single repository of our creative spirit.

These exercises strengthen the "creative thinking skills" described on page 30. They are a necessary complement to the skills you need to be excellent in the specific domain or field in which you work. To begin the program, turn to the next page.

GO TO PAGE 28

BIG C AND LITTLE C

CREATIVITY EXISTS when key elements come together: novelty, appropriateness, and a receptive audience in its field.

That last element, the audience, applies mainly to "Big C" creativity, the glamorous achievements of geniuses. But all too many of us do not see ourselves as being very creative—because we don't have much of an audience for what we do. In fact, we focus too much on "Big C" creativ-

Reliving the Eureka! Moment

START NOW with a basic exercise. We call it the "Great Idea" exercise. For this and the other exercises you may wish to record the instructions for playback or ask a friend to read them to you. Whenever there are instructions that should be either read to you or tape-recorded, you'll see this symbol ℰ.

We also suggest that you keep a journal for analyzing and reflecting on the process. If you don't want to keep a separate notebook, make notes in your calendar or datebook. Writing about your experiences increases the likelihood that you'll be able to recapture them. As you start paying more attention to your own creativity, it tends to become a beneficial habit.

ℰ Sit in a comfortable position with your back straight but not rigid, your feet flat on the floor, and your hands in your lap. Close your eyes and take a deep breath as follows: breathe all the way in to your belly and feel the breath filling up your lungs so that first your belly and rib cage expand, then your chest, and you can feel the air filling your body up to your shoulders.

ity and overlook the ways each of us displays flair and imagination in our own lives.

"We've become narrow in the ways we think about creativity," observes Teresa Amabile. "We tend to think of creativity as rarefied: artists are creative, musicians are creative, so are poets and filmmakers. But the chef in her kitchen is showing creativity when she invents a variation on a recipe. A bricklayer shows creativity when he devises a new way of laying bricks, or of doing the same job with fewer materials."

Still, much of what we know about our subject comes from the study of the creative giants. Howard Gardner has studied creative geniuses working early in this century, and notes:

"The amazing thing about Albert Einstein, or Sigmund Freud, or Virginia Woolf, or Martha Graham, is that they didn't just do something new. They actually changed the field or domain in which they worked forever after. But absent an initial curiosity and passion, which every one of these people had from an early age, and absent years of commitment, when they really took dancing or painting or physics or statesmanship as far as other people had, they would never have had the kind of creative breakthrough that changes a whole field."

Gardner believes that what is true about the Big C creators holds for the rest of us. Each of us has a bent for a particular domain. "Every person has certain areas in which he or she has a special interest," says Gardner. "It could be something they do at work—the way they write memos or their craftsmanship at a factory—or the way they teach a lesson or sell something. After working for a while they can get to be pretty good—as good as anybody whom they know in their immediate world.

"Now, many people are satisfied at just being good, but I wouldn't use the word *creative* to describe this level of work."

However, there are others for whom simply being good at something is not enough—they need to be creative. "They can't get into flow when they're just doing things in a routine way," Gardner explains. "So what they do is to set small challenges for themselves, like making a meal a little differently from the way they've made it until now.

"Let's say this year you decide to plant your garden in a slightly different way. Or, if you're a teacher, you say to yourself, 'I'm sick of writing student reports this year in exactly the same old way. Instead I'm going to give the student reports earlier and allow the kids to give me some kind of feedback.'

"None of these things is going to get you into the encyclopedia. You're not likely to change the way gardening, cooking, or teaching will be done in the future. But you are going beyond the routine and conventional, and they give you a kind of pleasure that is quite analogous to what the Big C creative individuals get."

CREATIVITY STEW

DAILY LIFE is a major arena for innovation and problem-solving—the largest but least honored realm of the creative spirit. As Freud said, two hallmarks of a healthy life are the abilities to love and to work. Each requires imagination.

"Being creative is kind of like making a stew," says Teresa Amabile. "There are three basic ingredients to creativity, just as there are three basic kinds of things a stew needs to be really good."

The essential ingredient, something like the vegetables or the meat in a stew, is expertise in a specific area: domain skills. These skills represent your basic mastery of a field. To possess these skills means that you know how to write musical notation, how to skillfully use a computer graphics program, or how to do scientific experiments.

"No one is going to do anything creative in nuclear physics unless that person knows something—and probably a great deal—about nuclear physics," Amabile observes. "In the same way an artist isn't going to be creative unless that person has the technical skills required for, say, making etchings or mixing colors. The ingredients of creativity start with skill in the domain—with the expertise."

Many people have a flair for something. "Talent is the natural propensity for being able to produce great work in a particular domain," says Amabile. "For example, it's highly unlikely that, given the kind of musical

Hold the breath for a moment and then begin to breathe out, starting from your stomach and continuing through your shoulders.

Do this twice more, each time holding your breath a bit longer between the inhalation and the exhalation.

You can use deep breathing at any time during the day when you begin to feel stress and want to calm your mind to be more creative.

Now return to normal breathing. As you breathe, notice that there is a split-second pause between the breaths. After you breathe all the way in, there is a pause before you start exhaling.

Then there is another pause before you begin to inhale. Keep noticing these pauses between the breaths. To heighten your awareness, try counting silently to yourself, "One, two, three..." during that brief period between breaths. Do this for a few minutes more, knowing that you can always do this to quiet the mind any time you feel the need.

Now in the open space of your quiet mind, remember a time when you had a great idea, one that solved a problem or dealt with a troublesome situation. It could be a time when you imaginatively resolved a bitter antagonism between friends, or a time when you conceived an ingenious way of childproofing a living room filled with antiques. Continue to keep your eyes closed.

It isn't necessary that anyone other than you considers this particular idea important, but it should have been meaningful for you. It may have occurred years ago or earlier today. The only requirement is that you felt you had a great idea.

Begin to mentally re-experience the whole episode in which you had the idea. Start by considering the time before you had the idea, when you had the problem but no solution. What was it like? How did you feel?

Now relive what happened when you actually got the idea, the Eureka! moment. What were the conditions in which the breakthrough took place? Take some time to savor that moment.

Next, take a moment to recall how your idea was put into action and the effect it had in resolving a problem.

As you continue to sit, search your memory for other ideas and solutions to problems you have had in your life, even if you didn't consider them at the time to be particularly creative. Mentally flag them as being what they really were: innovative and useful.

When you are ready, open your eyes. ✎

You can benefit from setting aside a little time every day to perform this exercise. The idea is to develop the habit of paying attention to your own creativity. Eventually, you will come to place greater trust in your creativity and instinctively turn to it when you are confronted with problems.

You might also want to talk about your creative moments with someone you are close to and trust. The enthusiasm in such a frank exchange can be astounding. This is probably because you are talking about some of the most emotionally charged and richest moments in life.

GO TO PAGE 50
↪

training that Mozart was given, just any child could end up producing the work that Mozart produced. There was something Mozart had from the start that made it easy for him to listen to music, to understand it, and be able to produce so much, so well, at such an early age."

But without training in the skills of a domain, even the most promising talent will languish. And with proper skill development, even an average talent can become the basis for creativity.

The second ingredient in the stew is what Amabile calls "creative thinking skills": ways of approaching the world that allow you to find a novel possibility and see it through to full execution. "These are like the spices and herbs you use to bring out the flavor of the basic ingredients in a stew," Amabile says. "They make the flavors unique, help the basic ingredients to blend and bring out something different."

These creative thinking skills include being able to imagine a diverse range of possibilities, being persistent in tackling a problem, and having high standards for work. "They also include the ability to turn things over in your mind, like trying to make the strange familiar and the familiar strange," Amabile adds. "Many of these skills have to do with being an independent person: being willing to take risks and having the courage to try something you've never done before."

Another variety of these skills has to do with sensing how to nurture the creative process itself, such as knowing when to let go of a problem and allow it to incubate for a while. If a person has only technical skills in a field—the first ingredient—but no creative thinking skills, the stew will turn out flat and flavorless.

Finally, the element that really cooks the creative stew is passion. The psychological term is *intrinsic motivation*, the urge to do something for the sheer pleasure of doing it rather than for any prize or compensation. The opposite kind of motivation—extrinsic—makes you do something not because you want to, but because you ought to. You do it for a reward, to please someone, or to get a good evaluation.

Creativity begins to cook when people are motivated by the pure enjoyment of what they are doing. A Nobel Prize-winning physicist, Amabile recalls, was asked what he thought made the difference between creative and uncreative scientists. He said it was whether or not their work was "a labor of love."

The most successful, groundbreaking scientists are not always the most gifted, but the ones who are impelled by a driving curiosity. To some degree a strong passion can make up for a lack of raw talent. Passion "is like the fire underneath the soup pot," Amabile says. "It really heats everything up, blends the flavors, and makes those spices mix with the basic ingredients to produce something that tastes wonderful."

Spicing the creativity stew.

AFFINITY AND PERSISTENCE

CREATIVITY BEGINS with an affinity for something. It's like falling in love. "The most important thing at the beginning is for an individual to feel some kind of emotional connection to something," says Howard Gardner.

Albert Einstein's fascination with physics began when he was just five, when he was ill in bed. His father brought him a present—a small magnetic compass. For hours, Einstein lay in bed, entranced by the needle that infallibly pointed the way north. When he was close to seventy, Einstein said, "This experience made a deep and lasting impression on me. Something deeply hidden had to be behind things."

Gardner believes such childhood moments are one key to understanding creative lives. "Without that initial love and emotional connection, I think that the chances of doing good creative work later on are minimal," Gardner says. "But the initial intoxication is not enough in itself. It essentially moves you to take steps to learn more about the thing that first interests you, and to discover its complexities, its difficulties, its strengths and obscurities."

From that initial love of doing something comes persistence. People who care passionately about what they are doing don't give up easily. When frustration comes, they persist. When people are resistant to their innovation, they keep going anyway. As Thomas Edison said, "Sticking to it is the genius!"

Deaf and blind, Helen Keller was cut off from the world and human

Helen Keller with Anne Sullivan.

AMERICAN FOUNDATION FOR THE BLIND, INC.

contact until Anne Sullivan came along. Sullivan's creativity lay in her passion and her refusal to give up. She was willing to persist in her determination to reach Helen.

Years later, Helen Keller recalled that first moment when that persistence, love, and passion bore fruit:

"My teacher Anne Mansfield Sullivan had been with me nearly a month, and she taught me the names of a number of objects. She would put them into my hand, spelled out their names with her fingers, and helped me to form the letters.

"But I didn't have the faintest idea of what she was doing. I do not know what I thought. I have only a tactile memory of my fingers going through those motions and changing from one position to another.

"One day she handed me a cup and spelled the word. Then she poured some liquid into the cup and spelled the letters: W-A-T-E-R.

"She says I looked puzzled. I was confusing the two words, spelling cup for water and water for cup.

"Finally I became angry because Miss Sullivan kept repeating the words over and over. In despair she led me out to the ivy-covered pump house and made me hold the cup under the spout while she pumped.

"In her other hand she spelled W-A-T-E-R emphatically. I stood still, my whole body and attention fixed on the motions of her fingers. As the cool stream flowed over my hand, all at once, there was a strange stir within me, a misty consciousness, a sense of something remembered.

"It was as if I had come back to life after being dead."

CREATIVITY IS AGELESS

THE POTENTIAL for creativity is always present. Creativity need not wane as life goes on. "Old paint as it ages sometimes becomes transparent," wrote Lillian Hellman. "When that happens it's possible in some pictures to see the original lines. A tree will show through a woman's dress. A child makes way for a dog. And a large boat is no longer in an open sea. That is called pentimento, because the painter repented, changing his mind. Perhaps it would be as well to say that the old conception was replaced by a later choice. It's a way of seeing, and then seeing again."

Bill Fitzpatrick rediscovered his creativity late in life. He is proof that what we are born with is always there—that one can see and then see again. In his retirement years he took up painting, something he had loved as a young man. Now in his eighties, Fitzpatrick has won many awards for his watercolors.

"I know too many people who just sit around waiting for the undertaker," says Fitzpatrick. "I think people who are going to retire should get involved in something that's going to take their time, their effort, and their thought.

"I'm eighty, but I don't think I'm eighty—I'm sort of a stiff, hurtin' fifty. I think it's important to live like that; otherwise you're vegetating."

As a child Fitzpatrick thought he would become an artist. But then the Depression came. Like so many others, he took the best job he could find. And so, for thirty-one years he worked for Nabisco as a driver. But through it all, he would work away at his painting, finding spare moments in the long working hours. That was why he began painting watercolors: it was easy to pick up and put down. When he retired he became more serious and started entering shows.

"People say, 'If only I had the talent to draw.' They've got it, I tell them. Because once you've got the urge and you start, it's all mechanical after that. The only thing that isn't mechanical is the creativity you use to think out your problems.

Bill Fitzpatrick at work.

"Creativity is very important in one's life—it gives you diversity. Being creative, you try different ways of doing things. And being creative, you naturally make lots of mistakes. But if you have the courage to stay with it despite your mistakes, you'll get the answer.

"I keep going and I don't have time to think about my troubles. I'm having a ball. Once you've lost that, I think you may as well pack it in. The main thing is just don't grow up!"

Erik Erikson, the psychologist who charted the stages of personal growth over a lifetime, described the triumph of the last stage of life as a "grand generativity": a deep concern for the younger generation and for generations yet unborn. Grand generativity is a wise and creative approach to nurturing others, an affirmation of life itself in the face of death. Often, the community at large is the beneficiary of the generative older person.

"Where'd Everyone Go?" a watercolor by Bill Fitzpatrick.

Now 100 years old and blind, Mary Stoneman Douglas continues her battle to save the Florida Everglades. She began her crusade nearly half a century earlier, long before today's environmental movement, with her book *Rivers of Grass.* In 1947 she showed that the Everglades was a vast yet fragile ecosystem that was already being depleted by agricultural irrigation and encroached upon by housing developments. Educating newcomers to the state about the continuing peril to the marshlands, Mrs. Douglas founded Friends of the Everglades and is now finishing her tenth book on the subject. "There is nothing inherently wrong with a brain in your nineties," she wrote in her 1987 autobiography, *Voices of the River.* "If you keep it fed and interested, you'll find it lasts you very well."

Pablo Picasso said: "Age only matters when one is aging. Now that I have arrived at a great age, I might as well be twenty." The creative spirit, far from declining with age, may actually gain in strength and vigor as an older man or woman—squarely facing the prospect of imminent death—concentrates on what truly matters.

Creative Lives and Tactics

PART OF CREATIVITY is in your way of seeing. When biologist Alexander Fleming came back from a vacation and found the bacteria in one of his petri dishes had died, he didn't simply regard it as a trivial experimental failure, as most biologists would have done. Instead he recognized that something significant had happened, even though it was not at all what he had been looking for. From his investigation of that "accident" came the discovery of penicillin.

Fleming's discovery illustrates what Yale psychologist Robert Sternberg calls "selective coding," the ability to sift important information from irrelevancies. Most of the information people get about a problem is of little or no use, while some is absolutely crucial; the key to creative problem-solving is being able to detect the relevant "signal" amid the irrelevant "noise."

Another path to creative insight is what Sternberg calls "selective combination," seeing a way to combine the relevant information once you've detected it. You may be able to pick out all the right pieces, but being able to put them together in a new way is a necessary step.

Charles Darwin put together facts that for the most part had already been known to other scientists of his day. His original contribution was to organize and interpret them in a way that lent support to his theory of evolution.

Another skill useful to creativity is the ability to draw comparisons and analogies. Many breakthroughs are the result of juxtaposing elements or ideas that ordinarily do not go together, or detecting a hidden pattern of connections among things. Analogies and comparisons help put things in a new context or help you see them in a completely fresh way.

> *"A person who never made a mistake never tried anything new."*
> — ALBERT EINSTEIN

In ancient Greece, for example, Hiero, the tyrant who ruled Syracuse, challenged Archimedes to say whether Hiero's crown was made of pure gold or had been adulterated. Archimedes knew what pure gold weighed, but the crown was irregularly shaped: how could he use this one piece of data to solve the conundrum without melting down the crown itself? The answer came to Archimedes as he was getting into his bath. Noticing the water rise as he lowered himself into the bath, the tale has it, he shouted "Eureka!" as the solution was revealed: he could determine the volume of the crown by seeing how much water it displaced, then multiply that amount by the weight of pure gold.

"You have to turn things upside down, view the world differently," says Peter Lissaman, one of the thinkers at AeroVironments, an innovative engineering firm that has come up with a long list of inventions. "It's as though you have a beautiful Persian rug, and you see a crimson rose in one corner and a deep red sunset in the other corner. But it's only when you turn the rug over that you notice that what you thought was the crimson and what you thought was deep red are connected diagonally by the same thread and are really the same color. They just looked different because they were surrounded by different colors. In seeking a creative solution, it helps to turn a problem over and look at it from the other side. Then maybe you'll discover the connections that have been hidden."

DARE TO BE NAIVE

THE ABILITY to see things in a fresh way is vital to the creative process, and that ability rests on the willingness to question any and all assumptions.

This ability is personified by Paul MacCready, one of America's most prolific inventors. His best-known accomplishment is the invention of the Gossamer Condor, the first human-powered plane to fly a mile. That triumph earned MacCready a $100,000 prize and won his plane a place in the Smithsonian Institution next to the Spirit of St. Louis and the Wright Brothers' plane.

"It's important to start with a clean sheet of paper—to have no preconceptions," says MacCready. "To design the Gossamer Condor, you had to pretend you'd never seen an airplane before. You had to figure out what was the lightest weight structure to make a wing that size, then figure how you'd keep it stable and how to propel it. But you didn't have to do any of this in the way anybody had ever made another airplane, because people who designed ordinary airplanes had a very different challenge. It's good to have some wide-eyed innocence.

"If you have too much knowledge of what didn't work in the past and what you think can't work, then you just don't try as many things. I was lucky: I had a good background in aerodynamics but none in aircraft structures. So it was much easier for me to come up with a very light and very large airplane, which turned out to be a good way to attack this particular problem.

The Gossamer Condor, the first human-powered plane to fly a mile.

STAY PLAYFUL

There is a paradox: Although creativity takes hard work, the work goes more smoothly if you take it lightly. Humor greases the wheels of creativity.

One reason is that when you're joking around, you're freer to consider any possibility—after all, you're only kidding. Having fun helps you disarm the inner censor that all too quickly condemns your ideas as ludicrous. This is why in brainstorming sessions in science and business the operative rule is that anything goes, and no one is allowed to immediately dismiss an idea as too absurd. People are free to generate as many ideas as they can think of, no matter how wild they seem. And in one of those ideas, there often is the seed that can eventually grow into an innovative solution.

Researchers report that when teams of people are working together on a problem, those groups that laugh most readily and most often (within limits—you can't goof off entirely) are more creative and productive than their more dour and decorous counterparts. Joking around makes good sense: playfulness is itself a creative state. As clown Wavy Gravy puts it, "If you can't laugh about it, it just isn't funny anymore."

"The Gossamer Condor didn't have to fly high or fast, so nobody got hurt if it broke. It just needed to be light. So you could make it very spindly, almost ready to break. And the only way you knew that you had the absolute minimum weight was if it broke occasionally.

"If it never broke at all, it was obviously overweight, stronger than it needed to be. Of course, if it always broke, you couldn't fulfill your mission. But if it broke about every twenty-fifth flight that was just right. And that's the way we designed it. Now, that's a terrible way to make an ordinary airplane. But it was very good for this particular vehicle. Breaking wasn't a failure; it was a success."

Asking the right question is crucial for creative insight. Says MacCready: "Once you've asked the question, people can come up with the answers. But you've got to pose the right challenge."

Einstein had the capacity to ask questions that were so fundamental that the answers transformed our understanding of the physical universe. As philosopher Alfred North Whitehead put it, "It requires a very unusual mind to undertake the analysis of the obvious." The prolific inventor Buckminster Fuller put it more bluntly: "Dare to be naive."

✳◎✳
THE ART OF LISTENING

GATHERING accurate information is essential to the early, preparatory stages of the creative process. The more good information you have about a problem, the better the chances of devising a solution. When the challenge involves other people, the art of looking and listening is all the more essential.

One subtle barrier to acquiring good information can be our social or professional role—that imposing persona we present to the world. In other words, who we are trying to be can get in the way of what we need to know.

One of the most intimidating professional roles is that of a physician. But Dr. Alexa Canady, a pediatric neurosurgeon in Detroit, listens with care in order to be more creative in her work. "My goal is to be the friendly neighborhood neurosurgeon," says Dr. Canady. "When people hear you're a neurosurgeon, there's a barrier that you have to counter. When you see me as a neurosurgeon, you're going to be nervous, you're going to forget what you came to tell me, your blood pressure is going to be elevated, you're not going to be able to communicate with me because you are intimidated.

"But most diagnoses in neurosurgery are made by history taking and by watching the patients and the way they function. And if they are functioning in an abnormal way because of the awkward situation in my office, then I have less insight into what is going on. Or if they are intimidated or too nervous, then they won't give me the information I need.

"So you want people to be comfortable, to tell you anything, even if

NO TWO OPERATIONS ALIKE

There is ample room for creative insight in medicine. Despite the solid science at its base, clinical practice is also a healing art with much room for flexibility. "People have this sense that medicine is specific, that if someone comes in with X, then we do Y," says Dr. Canady. "If you rationally analyze the treatments for about ninety-eight percent of the things we do, there is no controlled, randomized study to show that Y is better than Z. Surgeons come to have certain approaches through experimentation.

"In medical school, it all seems cut-and-dried until you do your first operation yourself. Then you real-ize that no operation is identical— not even something simple like taking out an appendix. No appendix is exactly the same as the last. What you find is that each person is unique: the anatomy is different, the disease is different. And how you respond is different, depending on what you find.

"You are always tinkering with

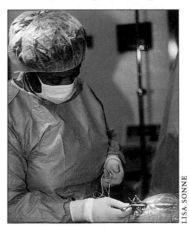

LISA SONNE

operations, learning from each procedure how to do it a little bit better, expanding your repertoire. Operating is fun, for a couple of reasons. One is that it is a little bit of a protected world. It is a time when you can concentrate fully on something without interruption. And there is a camaraderie in the operating room. It is a world where everybody is working together and you put your ego aside. And it's a place where you have to be creative.

"I think creativity is essential for life. It may be in how you interact with your kids. It may be in your hobbies. I think for many people the creativity in their lives is not in their jobs. But somewhere in your life there has to be a passion. There has to be some desire to go forward. If not, why live?"

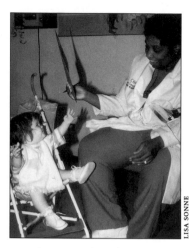

Dr. Alexa Canady with young patient.

they think it is going to be silly. I want to have a conversation with you rather than examine you. You have to see me not as a surgeon but as a person."

Says Dr. Canady, "I think the biggest part of creativity in medicine is listening. You have to listen to what the patient is really saying as opposed to what their words tell you. You have to listen to what the people who work with you are saying. Everybody who sees a patient has something to tell you.

"The nurse's aide can tell you something about the patient. We have a wonderful woman named May, who has taken care of lots of our children in coma from head injuries over the years. When you listen to May, you know exactly how that patient has been doing and when they are beginning to awaken. She spends many hours each day with them—and she has a much better sense of how they are doing than I do, coming during rounds for fifteen minutes.

"You listen to the parents because one of the things we find is that patients who are in coma often respond to their parents long before they respond to anyone else. If you stand there and watch the interaction, it is different—kids in coma will wiggle a thumb for their parent before they do it for other people.

"So you listen to anybody who knows anything, because you need all the help you can get."

LEARNING FROM RISK

CREATIVE PEOPLE ARE NOT ONLY open to new experiences of all kinds, they are willing to take risks. Jim Collins, an avid climber, is also a lecturer at the Stanford University Graduate School of Business. Although devoted to climbing, Collins spends much of his time on the Stanford campus, amid the placid rolling hills of the San Francisco peninsula. To stay in shape when he's so far from climbing country, he uses the buildings on the Stanford campus to hone his technique.

The stairs of the physics building or the walls of the historic quad-

KAREN HEILMAN

Jim Collins climbs the formidable California Beach Crack.

Collins experimenting on the physics building.

rangle courtyard become surfaces on which he can test and refine his skills. That way, when he actually attempts a difficult climb, his complex moves are well practiced. He doesn't have to figure them out when he's up on a really dangerous rock. His mind and energy are free for a creative breakthrough.

Says Collins, "Climbing is one of the most creative things I've ever done: it's constant problem-solving. There's no map to follow up a rock. You look at a blank cliff face and say to yourself, 'Potentially, there's a route up there.' But you have to invent it as you go along."

Collins says that climbing teaches him about creativity in business. Whether rock climbing or starting up a new business venture, "when you look from the outside you say, 'Gee, that seemed really risky.' Entrepreneurs often respond by saying, 'I didn't know it would work, but I got committed.' In business school we use decision trees—a very structured way of analyzing probabilities of something happening. The truth is, the probabilities change once you commit.

"In climbing, if you're bold and just go ahead and do it, when you run out of protection you think of the consequences of a fall. It's then that you start getting really creative, and working hard to stay on the rock. Here at the business school we're trained to keep our options open. But if you spend your life keeping your options open that's all you're ever going to do. You can't get to the top of the mountain by keeping one foot on the ground."

DOING THE IMPOSSIBLE AT PSYCHO ROOF

Jim Collins took up climbing while growing up in Boulder, Colorado, an area that has some of the most challenging ascents on the continent. Collins climbed for fun. But on July 28, 1978, Collins made climbing history. He became the first person ever to conquer Psycho Roof, a perilous rock in El Dorado Canyon, a world-famous climbing spot in the hills just outside Boulder.

There was one route up Psycho Roof that climbers knew from years of bitter experience was simply impossible. The problem was getting a perch on the lip at the top of the cliff. The angle at which the lip lurched outward blocked a climber's hands. The lip was just beyond reach of a climber's arm.

The solution: Collins realized he could turn himself upside down, hanging on to the side of the cliff just below the lip, and hook a toe on to the lip.

The advantage in the length of his leg over his arm made the crucial difference: using his toes like fingers, he was able to hold on while he reached up with his other arm and grabbed the lip. The impossible route up Psycho Roof became possible because Collins mentally "let go" of established patterns of thought long enough to approach the problem in a way that had never been tried.

☉* LIKE A COYOTE?

I N CREATIVE PROBLEM-SOLVING a mistake is an experiment to learn from, valuable information about what to try next. Indeed, many inventions have come about because of mistakes. William Perkins, a British chemist, discovered how to make artificial dyes while trying to create a synthetic quinine—a task he failed at. But he noticed that the sludge he had created in his experiment left a purple stain. Further investigation of this stain marked the beginning of the synthetic dye industry.

People often hold back in their efforts because they are afraid of making mistakes. They can be embarrassing, even humiliating. But if you take no chances and make no mistakes, you fail to learn, let alone do anything unusual or innovative. As an anonymous wag put it, "Don't refuse to go on an occasional wild-goose chase. That's what wild geese are for."

Research suggests that highly creative people make more mistakes than their less imaginative peers. The reason is not that they are less proficient—it's that they make more attempts than most others. They spin out more ideas, come up with more possibilities, generate more schemes. They win some, they lose some.

Chuck Jones, the legendary animator of Wile E. Coyote and Bugs Bunny, says, "I don't believe we learn by our triumphs. I think we learn by our mistakes. Goodness knows, it's not that you want to. But it's the stumblings that give us some clue as to what we're really driving for.

Animator Chuck Jones.

"The thing about Wile E. Coyote is that he's so much like all of us. The philosopher George Santayana describes the coyote perfectly: 'A fanatic is someone who redoubles his effort when he has forgotten his aim.' If that's not the coyote, I don't know what is." And what we admire in the coyote is that he keeps on trying.

No matter how heroic our efforts, the creative moment can't be forced; it comes to us naturally, when circumstances are right. Often, however, the demands and deadlines in our lives won't wait for the spontaneous emergence of insight. When creative energies won't flow on one problem

© Warner Bros. Inc. 1988

or project, it helps to have another to turn to, advises University of California psychologist Dean Simonton:

"Most of history's great creators didn't just have their hands in one basket. They would have lots of different things going on. If they ran into obstacles in one area, they put it aside for a while and moved on to something else. By having multiple projects, you're more likely to have a breakthrough somewhere...you're always moving along."

Leonardo da Vinci simultaneously immersed himself in architecture, painting, city planning, science, and engineering. While doing the studies that would found the theory of evolution aboard the *Beagle*, Darwin also made voluminous notes on zoology, geology, and even categorized facial expressions in humans and animals. Dr. Howard Gruber, a psychologist at the University of Geneva who has studied Darwin's creativity, calls such far-flung interests a "network of enterprises." He suggests that by shifting from project to project, creative people can bring elements and perspectives from one area that can help with another. It also means that if they've hit the stage of frustration in one project, they can put it on a mental back-burner while they turn to another.

✳◎✳

ANXIETY IS THE
HANDMAIDEN OF CREATIVITY

FINDING THE COURAGE to embrace your anxieties and take the next step is essential to creativity of all sorts. Chuck Jones knows it well: "Fear is a vital factor in any creative work. The fishermen from the Aran Islands off Ireland, one of the most difficult fishing grounds in the world, say that anybody who doesn't fear the ocean should not go fishing."

Jones confesses, "I've never made a picture in my life of drawing animated cartoons in which I didn't face this monster, fear. In live action it's a piece of film; with me it's a piece of paper. I've never finished one drawing without wondering whether or not I can do another one. Or whether I can even dare start another one!

"Anxiety is the handmaiden of creativity. But it's the recognition of the fear and the willingness to engage it that matters. Fear is the dragon and you're the knight. Any knight that didn't wet his steel britches before he went into combat wasn't a very good knight.

"I think that anxiety is vital. But the willingness to face it is what makes an artist. When you put your pencil down here and say, 'Now I know what I can do,' at that moment you are one with the gods because you realize that you do have the tools. Suddenly there's no more anxiety. Anxiety is the springboard that leads to your ability to join up with the gods that can draw."

Or, as Oscar Wilde said, "The anxiety is unbearable. I only hope it lasts forever."

©1991 WARNER BROS. INC, LJE INC.

Expanding Creativity

✺☌✺
FLOW: THE WHITE MOMENT

WHEN CREATIVITY is in full fire, people can experience what athletes and performers call the "white moment." Everything clicks. Your skills are so perfectly suited to the challenge that you seem to blend with it. Everything feels harmonious, unified, and effortless.

That white moment is what psychologists sometimes call "flow." This state has been studied extensively by Mihalyi Csikszentmihalyi, a psychologist at the University of Chicago. In flow, people are at their peak. Flow can happen in any domain of activity—while painting, playing chess, making love, anything. The one requirement is that your skills so perfectly match the demands of the moment that all self-consciousness disappears.

If your problem-solving skills are not up to the challenge you face, you experience anxiety, not flow. That's what happens when you find yourself taking an exam you haven't studied for, or are about to give a speech for which you haven't prepared. If your skills are too great for the challenge at hand, you experience the opposite: boredom. It's the feeling a Ph.D. in astrophysics might have if the greatest creative challenge in her day were arranging car pools.

When skills and challenge match, then flow is most likely to emerge. At that instant, attention is fully focused on the task at hand. One sign of this complete absorption is that time seems to pass much more quickly— or much more slowly. People are so attuned to what they're doing, they're oblivious to any distractions.

Csikszentmihalyi tells the following story about a surgeon performing a difficult operation. When the procedure was done, the surgeon looked around and happened to notice a pile of debris in a corner of the operating room. When he asked what had happened, he was told that part of the

"Creation" calligraphy by the abbot of the Koto-in Temple—a snapshot of the mind.

ceiling had caved in during the operation. He was so fully absorbed in his work, he hadn't heard a thing.

Neurological studies of people in flow show that the brain actually expends less energy than when we are wrestling with a problem. One reason seems to be that the parts of the brain most relevant for the task at hand are most active, and those that are irrelevant are relatively quiet. By contrast, when one is in a state of anxiety or confusion, there is no such distinction in activity levels between parts of the brain.

Flow states occur often in sports, especially among the best athletes. In his biography, basketball star Bill Russell describes those moments as ones of an almost supernatural intuition:

"It was almost as though we were playing in slow motion. During those spells I could almost sense how the next play would develop and the next shot would be taken. Even before the other team brought the ball in bounds, I could feel it so keenly that I'd want to shout to my teammates, 'It's coming there!' —except that I knew everything would change if I did."

NO-MIND

W HILE IN A FLOW STATE, people lose all self-consciousness. The Zen idea of no-mind is similar: a state of complete absorption in what one is doing. Says Professor Kenneth Kraft, a Buddhist scholar at Lehigh University who has spent many years in Japan, "In Zen they use the word *mind* in a very interesting way. The word is also a symbol for the consciousness of the universe itself. In fact, the mind of the individual and the mind of the universe are regarded as ultimately one. So by emptying oneself of one's smaller, individual mind, and by losing the individual's intense self-consciousness, we are able to tap into this larger, more creative, universal mind."

The idea of merging with the activity at hand is intrinsic to Zen. "It's taught in Zen that one performs an action so completely that one loses oneself in the doing of it," Kraft explains. "And so a master calligrapher, for example, is doing his calligraphy in a no-minded way."

Before the Zen calligrapher begins his first stroke, he pauses to bring himself into full awareness of what he is doing. That moment's pause is crucial to what follows. Instead of plunging pell-mell into the task at hand, he takes a moment to settle down in order to be at one with what he is about to do.

Inside Creativity

Gozan Matunaga, abbot of the Koto-in Temple in Kyoto, Japan, tapping into a more creative, universal mind.

BLACK STAR

No-mindedness is not unconsciousness, some kind of vague spaciness. On the contrary, it is a precise awareness during which one is undisturbed by the mind's usual distracting inner chatter. Says Kraft, "No-mindedness means not to have the mind filled with random thoughts—thoughts like 'Does this calligraphy look right? Should that stroke go there or here?' There's none of that in the mind if it's done by a master. It's just the doing. Just the stroke."

The making of a work of Zen calligraphy begins before the actual stroke. The master first composes his inner state. Only then does he turn to the calligraphy. From a state of no-mind, the first stroke emerges.

"A very important part of a work of calligraphy is the first mark that is made on the scroll, the very beginning of the character. It's from that beginning that the rest of it flows. If the beginning is off for any reason—if it's too deliberate or too timid or too bold—then the balance of the whole piece can be thrown off. People who have trained eyes can look at a piece of calligraphy and see very clearly the mind state of the calligrapher."

The works of calligraphy are so highly regarded as legacies of the masters who made them that they are brought out for viewing annually at many Zen temples. "They think of those scrolls as a kind of snapshot of the master's state of mind," says Kraft. "Some of the strokes are bold and heavy, some are wispy, some are very rushed, some composed and sedate. And yet all, in a sense, express the master's Zen, his awareness."

And in a profound sense, all of our creative acts express our awareness—who we are at that moment.

MIND LIKE WATER

IN THE WEST we often associate creative activity with invention and problem-solving, but Asian cultures traditionally take a somewhat different view. Creativity is seen as coming from a deeper source than innovative thinking. In Buddhism, for example, thinking is just one of the senses, and like all senses, it's limited.

"One of the goals of Zen Buddhism is to go beyond the senses and beyond thinking," says Professor Kraft. "Intuition—the source of insight—sneaks up on you from somewhere else when you're not thinking about it. You need to be receptive and responsive to this possibility.

"One of the images used metaphorically in Asia for creativity is water. Water conforms to whatever circumstances it's in. Water in a river rushes along, but if it comes to a rock, it flows around it. If you take a cup to the river and fill it, the water will suddenly and perfectly conform to the cup filled.

"By the same token, creativity is a kind of responsiveness to circumstances. A person who is deeply responsive to the conditions in which he finds himself will be very creative."

A mind as clear and reflective as water is central to the oriental martial arts tradition, which places a high value on responding to and even anticipating events. Enormous discipline is required to attain this state of mind, in which one is capable of receiving information without distortion. For it is accurate information—whether it is the detection of an opponent's next move in judo, or the anticipation of a subtle shift in consumer taste in automobiles—that forms the basis for creative action.

Letting Go

WHEN people reflect on those times they have been most fully creative and expressive, they often describe it as a "letting-go" experience. (See the discussion of flow and "white moments" on page 46.) It is at that point of letting go that creativity occurs.

It may be in doing vigorous exercise or in concentrating on some simple, repetitive task. It could be just as you are falling asleep, in dreams, or just as you are waking up. Many find that they routinely get a useful insight in the shower. Others have to take some kind of vacation, however brief, to surrender enough to free their creativity.

The view of creativity as a kind of dance of interdependence between observer and observed, or between producer and customer, has its roots in an ancient philosophy that sees all phenomena as interrelated aspects of a single, delicately interwoven system. Current scientific views of ecology mirror this philosophy, which holds that the most creative actions are those that are truly adaptive and responsive to one's total environment.

That channeling of creativity is seen in the art forms known in Japan as Ways: the Way of Calligraphy, the Way of Archery, the Way of Tea, the Way of Flower Arranging, or the Way of Judo. "These Ways are essential to Asian culture," says Kraft. "Initially to Westerners, it sometimes seems as if the Way is just a little narrow path, with very fixed rules and no creativity, and that your task as a practitioner of that art, whatever it is, is just to conform as best you can to whatever your predecessors have done.

"But it's more subtle than that, because no matter what circumstances you find yourself in, they are different than those of your predecessors. So even to conform to tradition involves adaptation and self-expression, and these are forms of creativity.

THE JOY OF JOY

Flow is an ecstatic state. It is joyful, a natural "high."

"What a lovely word *Joy* is," says animator Chuck Jones. "Whenever I think of Joy, I think that you just can't write it; it's got to be an elegant thing, with a pearl stuck in the top of it, all these little goodies down the side. And it's surrounded by an aura of happiness. It's really a pleasure to see Joy."

"And it's big, with a smashing *O* smiling at you. And it's lovely, like a *Yes;* you might say that the last letter of Joy is the first letter of Yes."

"And Joy is all decorated, all charming, with wings—by God, it can take off. And when you're drawing something and it works, that's the epitome of the whole matter. But without being willing to take a risk, make some mistakes, face the dragon of fear and keep going, you'll never know the joy of . . . Joy!"

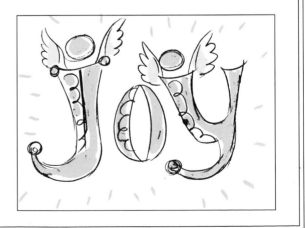

"In the Way of Calligraphy, for example, the character you write may be fixed—you can't alter the character—and yet it's remarkable how much variety different calligraphers will find in the identical character."

This is, perhaps, a more passive, more subtle way of thinking of creativity than the Western view of brand-new inventions and discoveries. But put to use, it can be a wellspring of energy and insight. The productivity and wealth of Japanese electronics and automotive industries spring from their mastery of creative adaptation and refinement.

MIND OF A CHILD

I N HIS STUDY of people who shaped the twentieth century with their creative genius, Howard Gardner found that although each of them had reached the limits of their domain—"Picasso at twenty could paint as well as anyone in the world; Einstein at twenty could do physics as well as anyone in the world"—they shared what seems to have been a childlike freshness in their approach to their work. "They captured something about what it was like to be a child, both in the sense of being a free explorer of a domain, somebody with the whole world open to them, but also puzzling about the sort of things children puzzle about," Gardner observes.

"Einstein asked what it would be like to travel in a beam of light. Many kids ask that kind of question, but few adults do. Picasso asked, 'What can we do if we take an object and break it down and fragment it into many different parts?' Freud asked basic questions about dreams. Martha Graham danced in the most formal, elemental ways.

"I think that every person—whether they are a Big C creative individual or a little c—is drawing on not just their knowledge and mastery of the domain, but something about what it was like to be a child—the kinds of questions and problems children confront all the time but which most of us are socialized to leave behind along with the other traits of childhood." Creativity first takes root in childhood, and the conditions under which it grows or is stunted are examined in the next chapter.

Meditating, stretching, playing an instrument, dancing, breathing deeply—these are other ways for people to surrender to their own creativity.

The following two approaches can also help move you from being stuck to letting go:

❧ Letting Go Physically. Sit in a chair with your hands resting comfortably on your legs. Tense your legs and keep them tense as you successively and steadily tense your pelvis, rib cage, shoulders, neck, and jaw. Hold all of that tense for a moment. Now relax.

You have just let go. How did it feel? ❧

❧ Letting Go Mentally. Imagine that something you mentally carry around with you—a strong emotion, belief, or thought that blocks your way—is actually represented by something you are wearing. It can be a shoe, watch, ring, scarf, bracelet, or tie. Imagine without doubt that this blocking mental set is contained entirely within the article you are wearing. The thought and the article have now fused into one. Then: take it off!

Observe what you are experiencing as you let go of this mental obstacle. ❧

GO TO PAGE 65

CHAPTER TWO

CREATIVITY IN CHILDREN

"There was a child went forth every day,
And the first object he look'd upon, that object he became,
And that object became part of him for the day, or a certain part of the day,
Or for many years or stretching cycles of years.

The early lilacs became part of this child,
And grass and white and red morning-glories, and white and red clover, and
*   the song of the phoebe-bird,*
And the Third-month lambs and the sow's pink-faint litter, and the mare's
*   foal and the cow's calf,*
And the noisy brood of the barnyard or by the mire of the pond-side,
And the fish suspending themselves so curiously below there, and the
*   beautiful curious liquid,*
And the water-plants with their graceful flat heads, all became part of him."

—WALT WHITMAN

WALT WHITMAN captures much of what we know about children and creativity: for the child, life is a creative adventure.

The most basic explorations of a child's world are in themselves creative exercises in problem-solving. The child begins a lifelong process of inventing herself. In this sense, every child re-invents language, walking, love. Art is rediscovered in a child's initial scrawl of a doodle she calls a "doggie." Sculpture begins all over again when a child discovers the delight of rolling a piece of clay into a shape that represents a snake. The seeds of mathematics emerge when that same child realizes that the clay in the shape of a snake is still the same amount of clay as in the original lump. The history of music unfolds the moment a small child first enjoys clapping her hands to a beat.

"The kernel of creativity," says psychologist Teresa Amabile, "is there in the infant: the desire and drive to explore, to find out about things, to try things out, to experiment with different ways of handling things and looking at things. As they grow older, children begin to create entire universes of reality in their play."

A washing machine is delivered in a huge cardboard box. Kids will play with the box for weeks, crawling in and out, curling up inside, inventing and reinventing the box: a bear's den, a gondola on a balloon soaring over the countryside, a pirate's ship, a space station, a grocery store—just about anything except an empty box the washing machine came in.

Our experience of creativity in childhood shapes much of what we do in adulthood, from work to family life. The vitality—indeed, the very survival—of our society depends on nurturing adventuresome young people capable of innovative problem-solving.

Parents can encourage or suppress the creativity of their children in the home environment and by what they demand of schools. Naturally, parents want to know ways to cultivate their child's creativity—to help preserve as much of their child's wonderment and spontaneity as possible. For the child anything is possible, everything is conceivable.

But the child's natural curiosity and delight are only part of the story. The more we learn about creativity, the clearer it becomes that it is a child's early fascination with a *particular* activity that paves the way for a creative life. This spontaneous interest leads a child to the sustained efforts and hands-on experiences that build mastery, whether at the piano, painting, or building Lego towers.

If we can avoid the narrow conception of intelligence and achievement that is traditional, there are many ways the creative spirit can be nurtured in childhood. But to do this we must begin with a basic understanding of human development.

The reason kids don't have to be taught how to be creative is that creativity is essential for human survival. Virtually every other species in the animal kingdom is born with a fully formed repertoire of reflexes and responses. Not so the human; we alone must learn and master from scratch almost everything we need to know to survive.

The brain and central nervous system continue to develop and mature through childhood and into adolescence. At around eight years the skull finally knits together, encapsulating the brain. But it is not until twelve or so that the brain achieves its full adult characteristics.

From birth through childhood, the brain has many more neurons than in adulthood. On the verge of puberty, the brain undergoes a process

IDEAS FROM
THE TWILIGHT ZONE

Brain specialists tell us that the brain-wave pattern of a preadolescent child in the waking state is rich in theta waves. These waves are much rarer in adults, occurring most frequently during the hypnagogic state, a twilight zone bordering on sleep, where dreams and reality mix.

Thus a child's waking consciousness is comparable to a state of mind adults know mainly during those dreamlike moments as they fall asleep. This may be one reason a child's reality naturally embraces the zany and the bizarre, the silly and the terrifying. A child's waking awareness is more open to fresh perceptions and wild ideas.

With puberty, the child's brain changes to resemble an adult's. The theta brain waves and the wildly creative flair of the child begin to fade.

Some people, however, continue to tap the richness of theta states later in life. Thomas Edison put the hypnagogic state to work when he was an adult. He had an unusual technique for doing this. He would doze off in a chair with his arms and hands draped over the arm rests. In each hand he held a ball bearing. Below each hand on the floor were two pie plates. When he drifted into the state between waking and sleeping, his hands would naturally relax and the ball bearings would drop on the plates. Awakened by the noise, Edison would immediately make notes on any ideas that had come to him.

called *pruning,* in which millions of neurological connections die while others settle into the patterns that will be retained throughout life.

One theory holds that those neural pathways used most frequently in childhood will survive the pruning more robustly. This suggests that habits set down in childhood have a remarkable significance for the potential of the adult. It gives a profound meaning to Alexander Pope's words: "Just as the twig is bent, the tree's inclined."

Nurturing Creativity

IF CREATIVITY is a child's natural state, what happens on the way to adulthood? Many of us will recognize ourselves in the sad tale of little Teresa Amabile, now a specialist in creativity.

"I was in kindergarten and my beloved teacher, Mrs. Bollier, had come to our home for an end-of-the-year conference with my mother. And, of course, I was eavesdropping on this conference from the next room."

Teresa was thrilled to hear Mrs. Bollier tell her mother, "I think Teresa shows a lot of potential for artistic creativity, and I hope that's something she really develops over the years."

"I didn't know what 'creativity' was," she recalls, "but it sure sounded like a good thing to have.

"When I was in kindergarten," she went on, "I remember rushing in every day, very excited about getting to the easel and playing with all these bright colors and these big paintbrushes we had. And there was a clay table set up where we had free access to all these art materials. I remember going home every day after kindergarten and telling my mother I wanted to play with crayons, I wanted to draw, I wanted to paint."

But kindergarten was to be the high point of Teresa's artistic career. The next year she entered a strict, traditional school, and things began to change. As she tells it, "Instead of having free access to art materials every day, art became just another subject, something that you had for an hour and a half every Friday afternoon."

Week after week, all through elementary school, it was the same art class. And a very restricted, even demoralizing one at that. "We would be given small reprints of one of the masterworks in painting, a different one every week. So, for example, I remember one week in second grade, we all got a small copy of da Vinci's *Adoration of the Magi.*

"This was meant for art appreciation, but that's not how our teachers used it. Instead we were told to take out our art materials and copy it. Second-graders being asked to copy da Vinci—with their loose-leaf paper and their Crayola crayons. An exercise in frustration!

"You don't have the skill development at that age to even make all

those horses and angels fit on the page, let alone make them look like anything. It was very demoralizing. You could see yourself that what you were doing was very bad.

"We weren't given any help developing skills. Worse, we were graded on these monstrosities that we produced, so we felt a heavy evaluation pressure. I was really aware at the time that my motivation for doing artwork was being completely wiped out. I no longer wanted to go home at the end of the day and take out my art materials and draw or paint."

THE CREATIVITY KILLERS

THE PSYCHOLOGICAL PRESSURES that inhibit a child's creativity occur early in life. Most children in preschool, kindergarten—even in first grade—love being in school. They are excited about exploring and learning. But by the time they are in the third or fourth grade, many don't like school, let alone have any sense of pleasure in their own creativity.

Dr. Amabile's research has identified the main creativity killers:

❋ **Surveillance:** hovering over kids, making them feel that they're con-

stantly being watched while they're working. When a child is under constant observation, the risk-taking, creative urge goes underground and hides.

● **Evaluation:** making kids worry about how others judge what they're doing. Kids should be concerned primarily with how satisfied they are with their accomplishments, rather than focusing on how they are being evaluated or graded, or what their peers will think.

● **Rewards:** excessive use of prizes, such as gold stars, money, or toys. If overused, rewards deprive a child of the intrinsic pleasure of creative activity.

● **Competition:** putting kids in a desperate win–lose situation, where only one person can come out on top. A child should be allowed to progress at his own rate. (There can, however, be healthy competition that fosters team or group spirit, as we will see on page 95.)

● **Over-control:** telling kids exactly how to do things—their schoolwork, their chores, even their play. Parents and teachers often confuse this kind of micromanagement with their duty to instruct. This leaves children feeling that any originality is a mistake and any exploration a waste of time.

● **Restricting Choice:** telling children which activities they should engage in instead of letting them follow where their curiosity and passion lead. Better to let a child choose what is of interest, and support that inclination.

● **Pressure:** establishing grandiose expectations for a child's performance. For example, those "hothouse" training regimes that force toddlers to learn the alphabet or math before they have any real interest can easily backfire and end up instilling an aversion for the subject being taught.

The Creative Spirit

One of the greatest creativity killers, however, is more subtle and so deeply rooted in our culture that it is hardly noticed. It has to do with time.

If intrinsic motivation is one key to a child's creativity, the crucial element in cultivating it is time: open-ended time for the child to savor and explore a particular activity or material to make it her own. Perhaps one of the greatest crimes adults commit against a child's creativity is robbing the child of such time.

Children more naturally than adults enter that ultimate state of creativity called *flow,* in which total absorption can engender peak pleasure and creativity. In flow, time does not matter; there is only the timeless moment at hand. It is a state that is more comfortable for children than adults, who are more conscious of the passage of time.

"One ingredient of creativity is open-ended time," says Ann Lewin, Director of the Capital Children's Museum in Washington, D.C. The children's museum is an arena designed to draw children into the flow state. But, as Lewin sees there every day, there is a marked difference between the rhythms of the children who come there and the adults who bring them.

"Children have the capacity to get lost in whatever they're doing in a way that is much harder for an adult," she says. "Children need the opportunity to follow their natural inclinations, their own particular talents, to go wherever their proclivities lead them."

Unfortunately, children are interrupted, torn out of deep concentration; their desire to work something through is frustrated. Lewin explains: "Adults have the compulsion to march through and see everything. But there are hundreds of things that can deeply engross a child here, things they can spend hours with. And you see the adults pulling them away, tugging at them and telling them, 'Enough, stop it, let's go.'

"It's a terribly frustrating thing to be stopped when you're in the middle of the process. But we live in such a hurry-up way. So again and again children are stopped in the middle of things they love to do. They are scheduled. There isn't the time for children to relax into their own rhythm.

Creativity in Children

"We adults are too pressured, too busy. I don't think our children have enough time—they're either overorganized or underorganized. You need the chance to stay with an activity for as long as it captivates your imagination, even if it lasts over days or weeks.

"A hurry-up culture means that again and again an adult steps in just at that creative moment when a child is heading toward mastery, and ends it. There are the bells at school, cutting off what you're doing. There's the pace of after-school activities. There are parents' schedules imposed on children's time. Children are hurried through their lives without the natural rhythm of unfolding. That, more than anything, will stifle creativity."

It's not just on outings to museums that adults' and children's timing conflict. Consider a child playing in a pile of sand. She puts the sand in her pail and dumps it out. Puts it in and dumps it out . . . puts it in, dumps it out.

"Her father, who just wants to get on with getting the cement laid, goes crazy watching her," says Lewin. "An adult has an end product in mind in almost any activity, and any action that doesn't take him directly to that end seems wasted and therefore frustrating."

THE MERITS OF DOODLING

MASTERY—one of the essential goals of childhood—comes through actions repeated over and over. That means practicing the small steps along the way, not worrying about getting results. Keeping a child's activities open-ended allows a child to do the same thing over and over in a variety of different ways and thus perfect whatever it is that they are trying to do.

Not only does repetition perfect skills, it allows the child to feel: this activity is mine, is part of me. And in the long run that may be more important for creativity than simple technical mastery. It allows a child to fall in love with the activity.

For instance, some children spend endless hours drawing cartoons on their notebooks, their textbooks, their desks—everywhere. Teachers and parents often see this as an aimless digression from more important activities. But there is another view.

The Capital Children's Museum once sent word out all over the city of Washington to find those students who drove their teachers crazy because all they did in class was draw. The museum organized several dozen of these budding artists into animation classes. It turned out that those endless hours the kids were spending doodling cartoons on their book covers and notebooks were not a "waste," as their teachers said, but rather an essential step in mastering a craft. The animation classes simply provided a setting in which that craft was appreciated, that practice valued.

Successful practice develops confidence, a belief in oneself. Stanford psychologist Albert Bandura calls that belief *self-efficacy,* the sense that one can master challenges. His research shows that people who have little self-efficacy are, understandably, timid. They have little faith in themselves or in their ability to succeed. They abhor risk; it frightens them.

But those who are confident of their abilities tackle something new with a strength that comes from having met and mastered many challenges before. That sense comes in large part from a history of accomplishments—riding a horse, playing the piano, solving a quadratic equation, writing a poem, acting in a play, and so on. For them the unknown is challenge rather than threat. They relish risk. They dare to try the novel, the uncharted, the completely original.

Self-confidence also depends on the feeling that adults—parents and teachers—respect one's ability. Constant criticism or steady indifference to a child's accomplishments can undermine the self-efficacy of even the most able child. Instead of a sense of confidence, the child is burdened with self-doubt and insecurity. All through life he will hear an inner murmur, the echoes of belittling remarks from childhood.

In short, the fledgling creative spirit feeds on encouragement and shrivels with criticism. Mastering a task is one way children build self-confidence. Knowing that they have been appreciated for doing a good job is another. It's best to judge a child's effort according to a child's standards, and give praise that will urge the child onward.

Four Tools

You have four powerful tools at your command to develop your own creativity:

*Faith in Your Own Creativity
*Absence of Judgment
*Precise Observation
*Penetrating Questions

Faith is a tricky word. To have faith in something, we mean here: to be able to rely on it without a second thought. To have faith is to *know* that you have a power within you that is always available to you. That is what your creativity can become for you, and faith in it strengthens its presence in your everyday life.

As St. Paul said in his letter to the Hebrews, faith is "the evidence of things unseen, and the substance of things hoped for." When people have faith in their creativity, they demonstrate a clarity of purpose that can startle those around them.

A second tool is absence of judgment. This is learning to silence that self-critical inner voice that censors your ideas before they reach fruition. Your "voice of judgment" or "VOJ" can make it hard for you to believe that you have had any good ideas at all. An effective way of shutting down the VOJ's negative chatter is to practice the breathing exercises on pages 28-29.

Now we come to the third tool: precise observation. This means seeing the world with the wonder of a child and the precision of a scientist. It means engaging everything around you with a refreshed awareness.

The fourth tool is your ability and willingness to ask penetrating questions. Some of the most penetrating questions are so-called "dumb questions." The inventor Paul MacCready reminds us, "The only dumb question is a question you don't ask."

In order to help you master these tools, we have created a set of exercises that you can adapt to your own schedule and needs. The exercises require that you incorporate into your daily life a particular guideline or rule of thumb. We call these guidelines "heuristics," which seems especially appropriate since the word has the same Greek root as the exclamation "Eureka!" so often connected to the creative moment.

We ask that you adopt one of these heuristics for a period of time—ideally no less than twenty-four hours and no more than a week.

For instance, to live with the heuristic "Pay Attention" (designed to strengthen precise observation) you might set your digital watch to go off on the hour to remind you to be fully aware of everything around you at that moment. The idea is to break set, suddenly fracture the routine consciousness that puts your powers of observation to sleep.

Another way of breaking set (especially if you spend most of your time in an office) is to find a quiet spot in a park. Just go out and sit for a while and allow your senses to take in all of the sights and smells.

GO TO PAGE 68

CHILDREN ARE NOT LITTLE ADULTS

CHILDREN ARE NOT little adults," says animator Chuck Jones, creator of Wile E. Coyote, the Road Runner, and a host of other famous cartoon characters. "But they *are* professionals. Their job is to play, their job is to experiment, their job is to try different things.

"When Mother says, 'Please be quiet, Junior, your father is very tired, he worked all day,' the kid legitimately can say: 'I played all day.' And that's what he is—he's a professional child in the same sense that a doctor is a professional doctor. And he is prone to mistakes just like a doctor is, when he forgets the forceps."

Because children do make mistakes, parents need to be very cautious in how they use criticism. A child's creativity can't develop under constant criticism, but the wrong kind of praise can be just as damaging.

"Parental love is not a fountain, it's a well. If you keep pouring it out and pouring it out, it loses its impact. But if it's there when the child needs to go and get some, it's much better. That way it's not what you need in your love for children, but what they need in their love for you.

"My parents loved me like that. Say, for instance, I happened to make a drawing and it had a lot of blue in it and some funny little figures. When I brought it in to my mother, instead of saying, 'What is it?' she would say, 'Gee, you used a lot of blue, didn't you?' " In that approach there's no criticism, just an honest reflection back to the child of what he's done. "There's always something you can observe about a child's drawing that has nothing to do with judgment," Jones says.

"Parents who don't know anything about art criticism feel perfectly fine criticizing their children's artwork. Equally bad is the parent who, every time a child comes up with a drawing, sticks it up on the refrigerator and says, 'That's wonderful.'

"But it isn't necessarily wonderful, and if you keep saying 'wonderful' all the time, the child subconsciously starts thinking, 'I don't trust this guy,' because the child knows it isn't wonderful every time."

Chuck Jones offers this example of the parent as art critic. Let's say a child makes a drawing of a flower:

"That's not a bad drawing," says Jones. "But most parents cannot put behind them the idea that they are critics.

"So the parent says, 'What's this? I suppose that's you?'

"And the little girl says, 'Yes.'

"And the parent says, 'But the flower is bigger than you.'

"Now that's the death knell right then. Because when you discover anything—when you look at it and you've never seen it before—then it seems much bigger than you are. It's enormous. It's like ants—they're wonderful. You get down on the ground, look through all the grass, and here are these enormous ants. So maybe the child is really being aware of a flower, really looking at it for the first time. And it's huge.

"Then the parent says, 'And what about this stuff?' The kid says, 'That's me, I'm dancing.' So the parent says, 'Yeah, but you only have one knee, you don't have all those.'

"That's nonsense. All you have to do is look when you're dancing. You feel you have ten elbows and fourteen knees and all kinds of ankles, all over the place.

"So when a child brings you a drawing, look at it and find out how it is different from other drawings. But also, don't look at the drawing, look at the child. If the child is proud of it, you have a right to sneak in on that pride—you'll become much closer to your child that way.

"But if the child is unhappy about it, don't say, 'That's great!' That doesn't make him feel better. He knows it isn't great. He may not be disgruntled, but he sure as hell isn't gruntled."

Faith in Your Creativity

CREATIVITY springs from inner resources that you have within you in great abundance. Faith in your creativity means faith in specific resources at your command. One is intuition, an immediate way of knowing something without going through a process of reasoning. You often experience intuition as a hunch or a sudden flash of insight.

Another is will, the strength you can muster to realize your goals. Creative people often have a compelling sense of mission that drives them forward even when the odds are against them. A third resource is joy, a sheer delight that can permeate an activity, making it its own reward.

We often talk about creativity in terms of breakthroughs. And to break through the wall of fear and criticism that threatens to stop you, you need to make use of a fourth quality: courage. Creativity entails taking appropriate risks, and courage allows you to use your intuition and will.

A final resource is compassion. This is what enables you to collaborate, to work with others, to value their efforts even when their results fall short. Compassion, when extended to yourself, helps quiet the voice of self-judgment

PLEASURE, NOT PRESSURE

CREATIVITY FLOURISHES when things are done for enjoyment. When children learn a creative form, preserving the joy matters as much—if not more—than "getting it right." What matters is the pleasure, not perfection.

For instance, many parents wish that their children would develop some kind of musical ability. Perhaps they regret not having learned to play an instrument themselves, and they don't want their children to miss out on the same opportunity. And so begins the childhood ritual of taking music lessons.

Unfortunately, that wish all too often goes awry: a child takes music lessons for a few months, or even years, and then loses interest. She says she doesn't want to practice the piano anymore. He complains that he's bored with the trombone. Or she says the violin is just too frustrating—that she hates it.

A better way is to follow, not force; let the child take the lead. Professor Teresa Amabile tells the following story: "I have some friends in California who wanted their child to play piano, and yet they were leery of destroying her love of music along the way, as had happened to them when they were both forced to take piano lessons.

"They did a brilliant thing: they rented a piano. This meant they didn't make a big financial investment, which is often part of the problem. Parents who have made this investment often wind up telling their children, 'By gosh, you're going to learn this thing. We spent a lot of money on it.'

"But my friends just rented, so they didn't feel that pressure. Their daughter was seven, and they took her along to help choose the piano, which gave her some sense of involvement in the whole enterprise. When they brought the piano home they didn't say a word about her taking piano lessons. Instead they said, 'Oh, Uncle Louie plays piano, and he comes over a lot. When he comes over, it would be nice to have something here so we could sing together and he could play for us.'

"Now, what's a piano to a kid that age? A big toy. Their daughter couldn't keep her hands off it. She was always over at the piano banging away. This went on for a long while, and it actually got to be a reward for her. Her playing got to be a bit too noisy, so she could only play at certain times of the day. And she'd watch the clock waiting for the hour when she could play.

"After a while she realized that she wasn't making music with it—it was just noise. So she asked her parents if they could teach her to play a song on it. But they said, 'Sorry, we don't know how to play the piano.' She'd try to sound out songs for herself, and get frustrated. And she kept asking, 'Can I learn to play songs like Uncle Louie does?' And her parents said, 'Oh, well, you need a piano teacher for that.' And she started asking for a piano teacher.

"When it was clear both to her and to her parents that this was something she really wanted to do, they finally let her start. And she loved it."

THE HOME ATMOSPHERE

IMAGINE A HOUSE where the door to the family room is covered with graffiti (e.g., "HOMEWORK STINKS," rendered by a child's hand in several lettering styles), a neon sign flashes "OOPS," the bathroom walls are papered with bizarre postcards, a bedroom door is plastered with bright decals. In addition, the house harbors board games by the dozens and books by the hundreds, a lizard and a fish, an electric piano, a pair of cats and a pair of dogs, a computer, a guitar, a quartet of hermit crabs, and a coil of snakes.

Eccentric? But maybe not atypical of many homes with lively, curious children. That is a partial catalogue of the surroundings of Jason Brown, whose play *Tender Places,* written when he was eleven, won a Young Playwrights contest and was later produced on television.

The catalogue of the things in Jason's house was made by Professor Amabile after a visit there to see the kind of family life that could give rise to such creativity. She found a home packed with the unusual and the

that discourages risk-taking.

Take a moment to consider what your life would be like if you could fully tap even a few of these creative resources.

Affirming Your Creative Resources

YOU'RE probably familiar with the psychological approach of creating an image of what you want to achieve before actually doing it. Tennis players, golfers, weightlifters, skiers, and divers all use variations of a technique in which they visualize what they are about to do before they do it. Using key words or images in their minds, they muster their will and affirm their intentions. Similarly, this exercise helps you to draw upon your resources and apply them to solving a problem.

This exercise won't necessarily produce instant solutions, but if done regularly, it will increase your preparedness for new ideas.

✎ Sit comfortably with your back straight and your hands in a relaxed position. Close your eyes and take a few deep breaths. Then breathe normally.

Notice the spaces between the breaths. Allow your thoughts to come and go without dwelling on them. Now let a problem or issue that is important to you take center stage in your mind. State the problem to yourself in a manner that is free of judgment and emotion. It is simply there in your mind's eye.

Now, either in a quiet voice or to yourself, say: "The intuition within me already knows the creative solution to this problem." Let this idea sink in. Imagine you even sense the latent energy of your intuition.

Breathe normally for a few moments. Then continue to the next affirmation: "Within me, in the center of my body, is an absolutely solid will, the foundation of everything I can do to resolve this issue."

Breathe normally for a few moments. Then continue to the next affirmation: "Within me is the capacity for joy. Allow the flow of this joy to carry me through the problem."

Breathe normally for a few moments. Then continue on to the next affirmation: "I have the courage to do whatever is necessary to resolve this problem." Continue to sit quietly and allow yourself to feel the presence of your courage.

Finally, affirm your capacity for compassion: "My compassion allows me to empathize with others, to forgive their mistakes as well as my own, in solving this problem."

As the thoughts about your resources come into your mind, allow your attention to settle on the problem or issue. Don't try to solve it but rather surrender it, gently offering it

curious, with the tools for creative expression always near at hand. Jason's home exemplifies the richly varied surroundings conducive to creativity.

But a stimulating physical environment is only part of the equation. Amabile—and many other researchers—have identified specific *attitudes* that also foster the creative spirit in the young. In creative families, there is a different feeling in the air; there's more breathing space. The parents of creative children give them what may seem to be a surprising amount of freedom. That freedom might even include collaborating with a child in pursuing a creative impulse. Consider the following case:

It is the 1950s. In a kitchen a mother stands opening cans and emptying the contents into a pressure cooker. Her son, a Boy Scout, wants to get a merit badge in filmmaking. His father had bought him a super-8 movie camera. Then the child got the inspiration to make a horror movie.

For one shot he needs red, bloody-looking goop to ooze from kitchen cabinets. So his mother goes out, buys thirty cans of cherries, and dumps the cherries into the pressure cooker, rendering a delightfully oozy red goop.

His mother is not the type who says, "Go outside and play; I don't want that stuff in the house." She is more than obliging; she gives him free rein of the house, letting him convert it into his film studio—moving furniture around, putting backdrops over things. She helps him make costumes and even acts in his films. When he wants a desert scene, she drives him out to the desert in their Jeep.

The goopy bloody kitchen scene, she recalled much later, left her picking cherries out of cupboards for years.

The son's name: Steven Spielberg.

Amabile cites Spielberg's mother as an example of the parent who supports a child's talent and passion: "Just imagine the kind of effect that this has on you, if you're a child. You're excited about something, you've got skills that you're just starting to develop, and you've got a parent who's allowing you to explore these skills fully—even if it means making a mess around the house."

That is not an easy lesson for many parents. "The main thing I've learned from my own daughter, Christene, about creativity is not to overcontrol, and how important it is as a parent to give her freedom and space," says Amabile.

"When she was really little, two or three years old, I'd see her playing with a new toy, for example, or a game, or just something she'd picked up somewhere. And she'd be trying to put something together or do something in a way that I knew was wrong: it wasn't the way the game was 'supposed' to be put together. And I'd rush in and say, 'No, no, honey, let me show you how to do it. It goes like this and like that.' And as soon as I did that, she'd lose interest.

"But if I just made opportunities available to her and let her wade in as she wanted, things were different. I just left all kinds of things around, stimulating things that she could handle, look at, play with. And I was available if she had questions. But I sort of kept myself back a little bit.

"I realized that she was discovering new ways of playing with games and toys. Maybe these weren't the way they were intended to be played with. But she was being creative."

up to the resources you have just affirmed.

Whenever you are ready, open your eyes. ✐

It's not easy to maintain an awareness of these resources as you go about your daily activities. So if you need a "recharge," run through the affirmations again. Also, the particular wordings of these affirmations are not etched in stone. They embody the seed of an idea, and you should feel perfectly free to express this idea in whatever words feel most comfortable to you.

GO TO PAGE 118 ↝

"YOU'LL NEVER AMOUNT TO ANYTHING"

Benny Golson, jazz musician and composer, remembers being passionately dedicated to music very early in life, almost to the exclusion of other things: "I didn't have hobbies. I didn't go to baseball games. I didn't do things the other kids did because I was home trying to learn about this thing called music. I remember a friend came to see me once, and I was busy practicing. He wanted to do something else and I wanted to practice.

"And when he left he made a very discouraging remark," Golson recalls, "about how I wasn't going to amount to anything anyway, so why was I wasting my time. But he didn't know that I *had* to do it."

Intelligence:
A Revolutionary View

WHEN PARENTS are supportive of their children's creativity, they will discover what psychologists are now confirming: most children have a natural talent, a flair for a particular activity.

A widespread but questionable view of creativity is that it is a singular capacity for originality applicable to whatever people do—a capacity that can be tested and quantified. That view of creativity is increasingly being challenged. Researchers now question whether one can do justice to a child's creativity with a paper-and-pencil test, which offers up a "creativity quotient" much like the score on an IQ test.

For example, one of the most common tests for creativity used in schools asks, "How many uses can you think of?" for objects like a junked car or some other everyday item. The test is scored for how many answers a child gives, for how unusual the responses are, and how many details are given for each. Giving a long list of highly original, intricately described ways the object can be used yields a high score on "creativity."

But many educators and psychologists, such as Howard Gardner, are skeptical of such measures of creativity. Instead of relying on a single test of creativity, Gardner argues that we should see how children respond to a wide variety of material that draws on varying areas of ability, including music, dance, and interpersonal relationships.

That approach avoids assessing creativity through a test that really relies on language ability. In this sense, the direct-assessment approach is an "intelligence-fair" way to assess creativity—it doesn't evaluate one kind of creativity in ways that actually demand completely different abilities.

Even with simple objects parents have around the house or can pick up at the store, they can get a sense of where a child's interests and abilities lie. By letting a child explore a range of activities, passions and budding talents are more likely to emerge.

THE SEVEN INTELLIGENCES

AN ESSENTIAL PART of the definition of creativity is that it is not only original and useful, but it occurs in a specific domain. This view highlights the importance of recognizing the areas in which a child's particular bent or talent falls.

For Gardner, a fruitful way to think about this is in terms of the many kinds of "intelligences." One's intelligence provides the basis for creativity; a child will go on to be most creative in the fields where she has the greatest strengths. Gardner identifies seven primary intelligences:

Language

LINGUISTIC intelligence is the gift of poets and lyricists, writers and orators—those who love language in any form, from James Joyce and Vladimir Nabokov to the masters of rap. One way to assess language skills in small children is by having them make up stories. A parent can do this by using homemade game boards, dolls, toy figurines, and small household objects to create an imaginary setting. This setting can then be populated by characters such as kings, queens, and bears and feature mysterious places such as caves and swamps. The parent can pose a question to the child: how does the bear entice the king into the dark, remote cave? The child then invents a story about how this comes about.

Not all children can or want to finish a story. When they do, Gardner observes whether they do it imaginatively, whether they play with sounds or create figures of speech, or just rely on humdrum combinations of words and routine scripts. "Some children who are not attracted by these imaginative stories turn out to be quite effective reporters—they are likely to use their linguistic intelligence to give accurate accounts in words of what they observe. Maybe they will work for their local newspaper someday," Gardner says.

Math and Logic

THIS TYPE of intelligence is exhibited by scientists, mathematicians, and others whose life is governed by reasoning. It has been particularly valued in the West, since the time of Socrates, and is even more venerated in the computer age. Most standard intelligence tests emphasize logic, the gift of such philosophers and scientists as Descartes and Newton.

According to Gardner, one way to ascertain this talent is by giving children a chance to test simple hypotheses. Gardner, for example, shows children that if you pour two different-colored substances together, they produce a third color. He then observes whether they explore further on their own—for example, whether they try to produce other color combinations and to figure out how they have been achieved. That is a clue that they are inclined toward logical thinking.

When it comes to numerical ability, the question is whether a child has an intuitive knack for numbers. Posing questions like "What's 2 plus 3?" misses the point. But some board games are good tests of the child's feeling for numbers.

Howard Gardner and his son Benjamin play the dinosaur game.

"In our research, we use a board game in which the child has to beat you getting from the head to the tail of the dinosaur," says Gardner. "The game includes strategy, where the child can not only play his own dice, but set yours any way he wants to. If a young child is able to set the dice so that, consistently, you lose and he wins, he is exhibiting both logical and mathematical skills."

Music

BY AND LARGE, youngsters who are gifted in musical intelligence are attracted to the world of sound, try to produce appealing combinations of sound on their own, or ask repeatedly for the opportunity to play an instrument. In a prodigy like Mozart, this ability flowers early and spectacularly; most professional musicians recall gravitating toward their craft in early childhood.

Kids' exposure to music at home is often limited to what comes over the radio or TV. Gardner advocates giving children the chance to explore sounds and create their own kinds of melodies. For example, there is a special set of bells, originally developed by education pioneer Maria Montessori. Says Gardner, "Playing with the bells lets kids explore the world of sound, to recognize what sounds like what: what's higher, lower, the same or different. What's scary and what's exciting. And then to see if they can actually create some little songs on their own."

Spatial Reasoning

SPATIAL reasoning is the knack for grasping how things orient in space. It involves the ability to appreciate visual–spatial relations—both those right in front of you, in the manner of a sculptor, and those covering a wider range, as does a pilot flying an airplane.

One of the earliest signs of this ability is skill in building things with blocks. Another is being able to imagine what something looks like from different sides—an ability that makes it easier to assemble and take apart mechanical devices. Being able to find your way around is another spatial talent.

It is not unusual to find a child who is doing poorly at scholastics but excels in working with mechanical objects. If you give such children an alarm clock or some other mechanical device, they will analyze it, figure out how to take it apart, and then put it back together again.

Having a strong spatial intelligence does not predict whether a person will be a scientist or an artist, says Gardner. But it does offer a strong clue as to the *kind* of scientist or artist someone might be.

Einstein had immense spatial skills. It was these skills that allowed him to use a "thought experiment," in which he imagined himself riding on a beam of light, to achieve a crucial insight in his theory of relativity. Leonardo da Vinci was also gifted with great spatial intelligence. Not only was he a spectacular painter, but his anatomical studies and the machines he devised—including tanks and flying machines—all display a strong spatial sense. Da Vinci also wrote poetry and songs, but nobody, Gardner points out, sings his songs.

Movement

IT MAY at first seem odd to consider the body as the locus of a form of intelligence. After all, Western tradition upholds a distinction between the mind and the body. But Gardner believes that the capacity to use your whole body, or parts of your body (like your hand), to solve problems or to fashion a product is as intellectually challenging an activity as figuring out cause-and-effect relations.

Basketball great Michael Jordan and the late dancer Martha Graham share a genius for movement, or *bodily kinesthetic* intelligence. Surgeons and craftspeople of all kinds rely on this ability to use the entire body, or parts of the body, to make something or solve a problem.

Most children begin to show their abilities in movement by using their body to solve problems—orchestrating winning plays in sandlot football, making up new routines for cheerleading, or whittling in wood. It is those children who continue to reason with their body, and to use their bodies in innovative ways, who end up as successful athletes, dancers, actors, or potters.

Interpersonal Intelligence

JUST AS WE tend to divide the body from the mind, we tend to associate intelligence with knowledge of the world of ideas rather than with knowledge of the world of persons. In fact, however, the ability to understand other people—what motivates them, how to work effectively with them, how to lead or follow or care for them—is crucial for surviving and thriving in any human environment.

"Traditional tests of intelligence ignore this knowledge of other persons, perhaps because the academics who designed these tests tended to be solitary thinkers," says Gardner. "But if intelligence tests had been invented by politicians or businesspeople, this form of intelligence would head the list."

NEWS OF THE
CREATIVE PAST

Well, we all know that creative people have a passion for what they do. Today this item comes from England where the budding young scientist Charles Darwin is recovering from a slight case of an upset tummy. It seems young Darwin was out in the countryside yesterday collecting rare insects. He noticed a strange beetle scurrying under the bark of a tree. When he stripped back the bark he found that there were three of these beetles hiding underneath. He became so excited about getting them into his collection that he quickly grabbed one in each hand and popped a third beetle into his mouth. Creativity can be all-consuming. Charles, we hope that tummy of yours gets better.

He adds, "Even in some very young children, a special sensitivity to others is evident. They are the ones who observe other children with great care or who are able to influence others to behave in ways that are desirable to them." And in the natural course of a child's day, this intelligence shows itself in how well the child gets along with peers and adults. In the course of playing, making music, or telling stories, many children give clues to this ability. One sign is being a natural leader—the one who leads the way in deciding what a group of kids will do next, or who smooths things over and settles disputes.

Interpersonal intelligence includes understanding other people—knowing what motivates them, what they are feeling, and how to get along with them. A child gifted in this area might show an unusual ability to empathize with another child who had fallen and hurt herself, or failed a test. In adulthood, it's the core of talent in fields like sales, politics, therapy, and teaching.

This kind of creative gift can spark vast social movements. Gandhi, the great Indian statesman, developed a strategy of nonviolent, passive resistance that drove the British out of India. It has been the strength and inspiration ever since of heroes like Martin Luther King, Jr., and the Chinese students in Tiananmen Square.

Intrapersonal Intelligence

INTRAPERSONAL intelligence is knowing oneself. A person with a high degree of intrapersonal intelligence knows his strengths and weaknesses, desires and fears, and can act on that knowledge in adaptive ways.

This intelligence shows itself in such things as having a decisive sense of preferences, or in self-discipline and the ability to persevere in the face of frustrations. Even young children display some self-knowledge.

Unlike other forms of intelligence, self-knowledge is likely to deepen throughout life. Encouraging children to be introspective—for example, to keep and reread diaries or journals—and to get to know people who are themselves contemplative or "wise," are all ways to enhance intrapersonal intelligence.

One of the great geniuses in this domain was Sigmund Freud. For decades he psychoanalyzed himself, paying special attention to his dreams and their meaning. And through a combination of his patients' free associations and his own self-analysis, Freud discovered truths about the inner life of people in general, such as the importance of early relationships with parents for relations later in life. In developing psychoanalysis, Freud came up with a method that can help people develop a stronger intrapersonal sense—a path to greater self-knowledge.

"This intelligence is often invisible," Gardner says. "It comes down to knowing yourself very, very well, and using that self-knowledge productively. There are people with very high IQs who just knock their heads against the wall and can't get anywhere with their abilities, because they don't really understand which sorts of abilities they have that might advance them, and what propensities get in their way."

APPRENTICES WELCOME

AN UNDERSTANDING of these areas of intelligence allows a parent to spot a child's natural areas of competence. Identifying these natural inclinations enables the child to explore them and slowly build a sense of competence, which can develop into an expertise. One day that expertise may become the launching pad for innovation.

Gardner offers a caveat: "It's important that parents and teachers watch children carefully and let them reveal their intellectual proclivities. Too many of us are narcissistic: either we expect our children to do just what we did, or we insist on their doing what we could not do or did not have the chance to do. Both of these paths are destructive, because they involve substituting the parent's will for that of the developing child." As archi-

Creative problem-solving at eighteen months.

tects of the home environment, parents can expose children to a wide range of materials and experiences so that a child's natural bent can emerge, no matter in which area it might lie.

Of course, it may not be enough for children just to investigate an interest on their own. No matter how talented a child is as an artist, for instance, she can pick up much worth knowing about the techniques of art from someone who is well versed in painting. But what can a parent do when a child shows a passion for something about which the parent knows absolutely nothing? There aren't always after-school classes in astronomy, weaving, bug collecting, chess, or building model airplanes.

The old apprenticeship system, observes Gardner, provided such mentoring for young people. "Long before we had schools, kids would learn a craft by being with adults in a shop or farm and being told what to do to help out. It might start out with just sweeping the floors, but after a while it might be trimming the fabric, then doing a bit of sewing. And after five or six years, you'd have a budding tailor."

Michael Spock of the Field Museum in Chicago has a bright idea: match a child who has a burgeoning fascination in a subject with an older person who has mastered it. Right now there is no easy way to do this. But, Spock proposes, just as there are decals for charge cards on the front doors of businesses, people who have special expertise they'd like to share with children could have similar signs on their doors. It might be a little chessboard, telescope, or loom—like the signs that craftsmen hung out in the old days of crafts and guilds. That way children in a neighborhood would know which adults had what skills, and who was open to teaching them about it.

This would be a delight for many retired people, who have plenty of time to spare and lots of skills to pass on to eager children. And, adds Howard Gardner, "it would link the generations with the kind of communal glue that is fast vanishing."

As the world community matures in the post–Cold War era, there may actually be a renewed interest in the benefits of mastery and the traditions of apprenticeship. The suppressed creative energies of former Communist countries could be released, generating a new wave of innovation and high-quality craft. Economic relations between the United States, Japan, and Europe could evolve into a stable system based upon continuous, creative competition. One result of this more evolved global community could be a move away from the current "quick fix" mentality and toward a longer, more patient view of human development and learning. In this view, value is placed upon the unforced emergence of both individual and group creativity, with special regard for the natural and spontaneous mind of the child.

Playful Schools That Work

CREATIVITY—ITALIAN STYLE

REGGIO EMILIA is a community in northern Italy not far from Milan. For the last forty or so years some of the most innovative work in early childhood education has gone on there in a "play school" attended by children from two to six. The school borrows from the Montessori approach, as well as from Piaget's studies of the developmental changes children experience. But it is a blend all its own, with a unique emphasis on individual spontaneity and group effort.

Children there are given enormous scope in the resources they can draw on: they spend much time out of doors, visiting a variety of places—from farmers' fields to ancient piazzas—and they have a rich set of materials in the school itself. The school staff knows the kinds of problems and puzzles to pose at different ages that mobilize the children's energy and attention, and draw them into meaningful projects. Working on such projects—whether a drawing, sculpture, or some kind of scientific experiment—shows children that if they work on something every day, they get better and produce something they are proud of and that other people appreciate, too. The Reggio Emilia approach weds

At play in a field of poppies—into the realm of the creative spirit.

COURTESY OF COMUNE DI REGGIO EMILIA

Expressing the poppy field experience.

children's natural curiosity with the social satisfactions of collaborative effort.

One special aspect of the school is the total involvement of parents. In fact, the Reggio Emilia school was created after World War II by a group of parents who joined together and took over an old movie theater. Eventually, when the municipality offered to support its programs, the parents were adamant that the spirit of their involvement not be lost. One parent recalls, "We saw the participation of the family as a right, a duty the family has toward the school." To this day parents take pride in the fact that it is *their* school, not the municipality's or the government's.

As one mother says, "We wanted a new kind of school, a new image of what the child is and can be. People in this town feel that what you do for young children is a kind of investment for the future."

Like many cooperative schools, Reggio Emilia weaves parents into as many of its activities as possible. "As a parent I believe we should not delegate the education of our children to the school," says Tiziana Filippini, a parent and project leader at the school. "That's what I liked about this school. From the first day I brought my daughter Eliza here I was asked to participate, to be involved in every way."

The teachers, says Tiziana, "start involving you even before the children arrive in September. The teachers will meet with you and ask about your daughter or son. They ask you to come to the school and to prepare surprises—toys, cookies, little gifts—to give the children for the first few days."

Parents of each class meet regularly, to talk over their children's development, deal with problems, come up with new ideas for the children.

The Creative Spirit

"It helps you as a parent be more fully involved in the growth of your child," Tiziana finds.

Niente Senza Gioia

NIENTE SENZA GIOIA—"Nothing Without Joy"—is one of the school's guiding maxims. Every effort is made to keep school a delight for children, right from the first day.

"I believe that children expect from adults the capacity to offer joy," says Loris Malaguzzi, education director of the District of Reggio Emilia. "They ask it of everyone and everything. Without truly radiating and receiving joy, an adult cannot foster an atmosphere where children can invent and create."

Malaguzzi likens fostering the creative process to growing mushrooms. "There are so many kinds of mushrooms: beautiful ones that are not good to eat, mushrooms that are not so beautiful but are wonderful to eat, some that are both and some that are neither. To grow the best mushrooms, the main thing you can do is to prepare as fertile a field as possible. And if they grow, they grow."

And that, he says, is what happens with the children at Reggio Emilio: they are given ample opportunity for their creativity to sprout.

"Creativity is a kind of continuously evolving fantasy, and you don't know when a child will grab at that fantasy," says Malaguzzi. "What we like to do is to accompany a child as far as possible into the realm of the creative spirit. But we can do no more. At the end of the path is creativity. We don't know if the children will want to follow the path all the way to the end, but it is important that we have shown them not only the road, but also that we have offered them the instruments—the thoughts, the words, the rapport, the solidarity, the love—that sustain the hope of arriving at a moment of joy."

Niente senza gioia—a mobilization of energy and attention.

One way children are escorted into the realm of creativity at Reggio Emilia is through careful attention to the first buds of curiosity. Tiziana

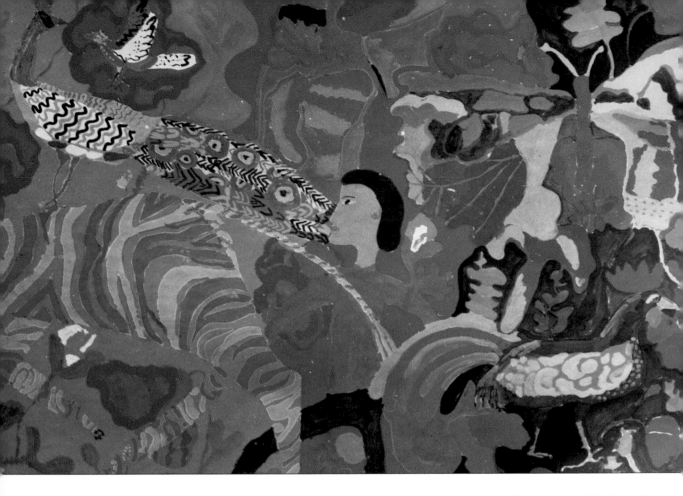

A group work by preschoolers in Reggio Emilia.

explains that instead of simply imposing some "creative activity" on the children, the school starts from a need or desire of the child.

Poppy Fields and Murals

THE CURRICULUM at Reggio Emilia is not built around subjects, but around projects involving a collective effort. The children are immersed in an activity, whether it be tracing a stone lion in the town square or going to a field of poppies and re-creating in art the sensory richness of that field.

In the spring, the hills around Reggio Emilia become bright red and green carpets of poppies, a brilliant harbinger of the summer to come. A child brings to school a big bouquet of dazzling red poppies. That fires the enthusiasm of her schoolmates. Where do the poppies come from? How do they grow? To pursue these questions, a trip to the poppy fields is organized for a coming day.

Once there, the children romp freely. They pick the flowers, run around the field, entwine flowers in their hair, hide amid the tall stalks, examine bugs. As one ecstatic little boy put it, "This is better than ice cream!"

Back at the school, poppies become a theme for further exploration. Slides taken by a teacher are projected onto a screen and children dance in and out of the bright images, washing themselves in color. Then a teacher proposes that they do a giant, collaborative mural inspired by the trip to the poppy field. The mural, Tiziana observes, "is a kind of big puzzle in which each child, according to his sensibility, has to make a special effort to contribute to a beautiful group work. This means using your individual spirit, but also taking in what the group can give to you, so that your thinking will be much richer than it was before."

Teamwork is one of the main lessons for kids at Reggio Emilia. "We try to develop creativity both in the individual and also in groups. Working in a group can help you produce something more, to think more widely, to enrich you. So we are concerned about creating a spirit of collaboration," says Tiziana. In making the poppy mural, says Malaguzzi, "the children began first by working alone, to delineate the single part that they would bring to the fresco. Then they meet and discuss each other's ideas, to decide how to put them together. That way they learn how something made by many people can truly work."

The process of making the mural matters as much as the final product. "It's not just the images that come from the hands and imagination of the children that count, but also the dialogue that takes place among them while they paint. I would say every stroke is the fruit of the individuality of the child, and also the fruit of the harmony of all their ideas," notes Malaguzzi.

"To place the colors, to find the right balance in a symphony of colors," he adds, "means for the child to become the extraordinary instrument of an orchestra."

"From a parent's point of view," says Tiziana, "we are also concerned about children not losing their individuality." Projects like the poppy mural show children that collaboration can extend their individual efforts. The result is a work of scope and complexity beyond what any individual child could produce—something the whole community can especially value.

The projects at the Reggio School draw on a range of intelligence:

spatial, movement, musical, and the like. Most schools focus on just two kinds of intelligence: language and math or logic. "These subjects are put at the top of the pyramid," Gardner says. "If you're good in language and logic, you'll do fine in school, and think you're very smart and very creative. And as long as you stay in school, it will be a self-fulfilling prophecy, since those are the two intelligences that are used to tell if someone is smart in school.

"That's fine if you stay in school all your life, or become a professor like me. But most of us eventually leave school and walk out into the world. At that point much of what was stressed in school is less relevant: most of what people do in life does not require the language/logic blend, and most of the ways people work together—including working together creatively—are not particularly focused on language and logic.

"Ordinary schools are an excellent device for training certain kinds of skills and certain kinds of people—especially teachers and professors. But they fall way short when you think about the range of human intelligence."

In short, exposure to a wider range of skills than is offered in ordinary schooling would not only tease out the natural talents in children. It would also be a broader, and better, preparation for life.

☙*

BEYOND REPORT CARDS

THERE IS A remarkable elementary school in an inner-city neighborhood in Indianapolis called the Key School. It is a school where Howard Gardner's vision of creativity is an integral part of the curriculum.

Each day every child is exposed to materials designed to stimulate the whole range of human abilities—in art, music, computing, language skills like learning Spanish, mathematics, physical games. Beyond that, attention is paid to personal intelligence, knowing oneself and knowing others.

Like other public schools, the Key School is open to any child in Indianapolis, although it is so popular that its students must be chosen by lottery. The teachers at the Key School are chosen with an eye to unique qualifications. Above and beyond normal teaching experience, teachers there are prized for their special abilities in the various areas. One teacher, for example, is excellent at signing in the language of the deaf—a skill in both the linguistic and kinesthetic domains.

The Key School's aim is to let children discover those domains where they have natural curiosity and talent, and allow them to explore them. Gardner explains: "The idea of this school is not that you should discover the one thing a child is good at and insist he or she focus only on that. By virtue of the fact that the kids are exposed to everything every day, they have lots of opportunities to change their minds and go in new directions. I think that reduces the likelihood that any child will come to that really tragic conclusion: I'm not good in anything.

"As long as we're just asking for a narrow band of scholastic performance—completing a workbook where you fill in the blanks, or a stan-

Children of the Key School form "pods" to pursue activities of special interest to them.

dardized test where you have to make sure that you put the mark in the right place—an awful lot of kids are going to come to the conclusion that they just don't have what it takes.

"But if you give kids a chance to use their bodies, their imaginations, their different senses, the chance to work with other kids, almost everybody will find out that he or she is good in something. And even the child who isn't outstanding in some area still has relative strengths. Rather than give that child the conventional message, You're dumb, the thing to say is, You're pretty good in these things; let's put more energy and effort into them."

To enable the child to pursue activities that bring a sense of accomplishment and pleasure, the Key School has created a relatively unstructured play area called the "Flow Center." The Flow Center draws on the ideas of Professor Mihalyi Csikszentmihalyi of the University of Chicago (see page 46). In a flow state, a child (or an adult) is so thoroughly and enjoyably engaged in an activity that nothing else seems to matter. The separation between the doer and the doing vanishes. There exists a state of complete absorption in which all self-consciousness disappears.

Three days a week, children at the Key School visit the flow room to play with a variety of games, puzzles, and objects. What the child does in the flow room is done for its own sake—not because the task is assigned. There are no grades, no "good" or "bad" evaluations. A teacher takes note of the degree to which a child is engaged in an activity. This is actually a record of the child's intrinsic motivation, and an indication of what the child truly enjoys and might continue to pursue later in life.

Every nine weeks there are different themes, like Patterns, or Connections, or more specific topics, like the Renaissance in sixteenth century Italy and "Renaissance Now" in Indianapolis. Each child then designs a project related to the theme. The projects aren't graded. Instead, each child presents them to her classmates, explains them, and answers questions. The whole process is videotaped, so that all the children in the Key School end up with a record of their growth and development through the years.

Both the Reggio Emilia School and the Key School champion collaboration and teamwork. The lesson learned from such collaboration is that the whole is greater than the sum of its parts. By working together, children see that they can make up for their own deficits and offer other children their own strengths.

Pods

AT THE Key School each child, every day, can choose from among activities that draw on the seven intelligences. This allows the child to explore undeveloped areas of interest, and to work more intensively on areas of strength.

Every child participates in a "pod," a special interest group. There are pods on gardening, architecture, gliding, and so on. One year there was even a pod on making money. Children choose the pod they want to be in, and every day they join other kids of all different ages, along with an adult, to explore that topic. The pod becomes a kind of apprenticeship.

All the pods draw on several intelligences, since few activities in life

---

COLLABORATION IS A TEAM SPORT

The Basketball Hall of Fame is in Springfield, Massachusetts, the city where James A. Naismith invented the game. What few people realize, though, is that though he got the credit, the invention of this ultimate team sport was itself a team effort.

In the 1880s Springfield College was a hub for physical education, the place where coaches from YMCAs all over the country came to improve their skills. In the fall, the game everybody loved was football. But when winter's snows came, sports had to move inside, where the only activities at the time were calisthenics. Boring, the students complained.

Naismith went to the dean and pleaded for a two-week break from calisthenics to concoct a new indoor winter game. So Naismith and his students began an intense period of experimentation, with themselves as guinea pigs. Indoor football, they soon learned, was far too rough. The same was true of soccer and lacrosse, the other popular games of the day. They needed a game that would minimize roughness—hence the rule that players could not touch each other, that the ball could be touched with hands only, and that players could not run holding the ball. And no bats or sticks—that was asking for trouble inside a gym. The players would have to pass the ball to each other.

And so, day after day, Naismith and his students, through trial and error, steadily refined the game.

At the end of the two weeks, when the first fully developed basketball game was played, the only hitch was that whenever a score was made, the whole game ground to a halt while someone climbed a ladder to get the ball out of the peach basket they had fastened to the gym balcony. But that wasn't such a terrible problem that first time out: the score was just 1–0.

---

demand just one. For example, the ethnic dancing theater pod relies primarily on a bodily kinesthetic ability. But it also draws on language and spatial intelligence. In the sing and sign pod children learn to use sign language along with the words in the songs they sing—an experience that calls on musical, linguistic, bodily kinesthetic, and interpersonal abilities.

By immersing children in activities they naturally take to, the Key School sets the stage for what Howard Gardner calls "crystallizing experiences": exposure to a person, idea, or activity that completely captures their attention and imagination. From such a crystallizing experience can grow a life's work.

The continual effort to stimulate the imagination and interest of the child is at the core of the Key School's educational philosophy. "What we are trying to trigger here," says principal Patricia Bolanos, "is as many flow experiences for children as possible. Because out of that comes the desire to do more and to learn more, and to take on yet another challenge. If the kids just stay at the same level of development in whatever they are doing, they get bored. We don't want anyone to be bored around here; there is no reason for boredom ever to set in. As soon as they master one area, they can go on to the next challenge. And it shouldn't stop here at school; it should become a style for life."

For that reason teachers at the Key School are on the lookout for those activities to which a child seems particularly drawn. In fact, the degree of motivation is so important that it becomes part of the child's school records.

"Most schools are predicated on rewarding students for doing the things they ought to do," says Bolanos. "We've turned that around completely. We are saying that instead of coercing kids to do things, you give them chances to be involved in activities they relish."

Children's Museums

COMPLETELY ABSORBED, a little girl pulls the "devil's tail"— the long handle that operates a sixteenth-century printing press. She pulls it over and over again, with increasing vigor and authority. Swathed in a serape, an inner-city child tastes a sweet Mexican chocolate drink for the first time. A goat indulges the tentative patting of a shy young boy. Not far away, another child peers into the whirling drum of a zoetrope.

The setting is the Capital Children's Museum in Washington, D.C. Children's museums are relatively new. In the 1970s there were only a handful, but in the last decade three hundred have sprung up in the United States alone. A children's museum is defined not only by its target audience, but by the artful combination of entertainment with education. It is a child-friendly environment filled with the kind of mechanical devices and elaborate displays that few schools can afford.

Mastering the printing press at the Capital Children's Museum.

Children's museums serve as an antidote to larger forces that oppress children. For middle-class kids there is the frantic pace of back-to-back classes, afterschool activities, and homework that mirrors adult time pressures. For inner-city kids it's the atmosphere of poverty, violence, and fear. Add to this the fact that children spend more and more time settled in front of a television set, and less and less getting to know a variety of different people, and seeing how the world really works. "These days even the toys play themselves; the child doesn't have to bring anything to them," says Ann Lewin, director of the Capital Children's Museum. "But the first thing you need for creativity is to feed a child with richness of experience."

"It's almost as if we have to reinvent childhood," she continues. "The society is out of synch with what a child needs to grow up healthy. We need to find new ways that enable children to grow up whole, to allow creativity to flower, to let childhood be childhood again."

⟨◉⟩
WHERE DOES MILK COME FROM?
CARTONS, OF COURSE

L ARGELY THROUGH TELEVISION, children today have more information about a greater variety of places and things, but have much less in-depth experience. In a real sense, children know more but understand less. The hands-on experience children had in earlier times with agriculture and crafts made clear to them that life is a process of doing, and that a process has a beginning, a middle, and an end. Through its quick succession of images and compression of time, television destroys this sense of process, conveying the illusion that things just "happen."

Children rarely have the chance to see where the things they use come from, much less how they're made. "Sodas arrive in a can, or food comes in packages that you stick in a microwave," says Lewin. "Children have no way to gain an appreciation for the time and labor that's involved in growing crops or raising the cows that provide the milk they drink."

"Kids come into our museums who have never had contact with a common farm animal, or have no idea how things are made," Lewin finds. The work that people did, which was always so much a part of a child's ordinary experience, has largely disappeared from view in a few short generations. Farms and factories are vanishing. What once was commonplace is now rare: neighborhoods used to have local bakeries, tailors, and repair shops for everything from appliances to dolls.

One way the Capital Children's Museum shows process is by an exhibit that re-creates a miniature clothing factory. Children can follow the bolts of fabric as they arrive, go through a layout of the pattern, through the cutting room and on to the sewing room. And, finally, the clothes are put on hangers, boxed, and loaded on a truck at the other end of the factory. The exhibit fills in all the mysterious steps that take place before the clothes appear on a rack at the store—the only way most kids have ever seen them.

LANGUAGE AND SPACE

T THE CAPITAL CHILDREN'S MUSEUM, one wing is given over to re-creating aspects of Mexican life—from a Oaxacan kitchen to a village well. Rooms and buildings on many levels are connected by a maze of ramps, stairs, balconies, doors. But there are no official paths to follow through this complex exhibit. A child has to figure it out on his own. "This space calls into play spatial intelligence," points out Lewin. "Spatial intelligence is virtually left out of formal education. In kindergarten we give children blocks and sand with which to build. Then we take those things away for the next twelve years of their education and expect kids to be architects and engineers."

Discovering the birth of communication in the Children's Museum's Ice Age Cave.

A child's mastery of the words, pictures, and gestures used for expressing ideas is essential for creativity. At the museum, children can journey through a series of environments, each of which represents a different stage in the evolution of human communication—from cave art to video animation. The exhibits mark the history of technological progress up to today's electronic media in a way that allows the child, step by step, to understand the nature of communication.

The child wanders into the dark and shadowy interior of a simulated Ice Age cave. Splashes of light on the rough walls reveal brilliantly colored drawings of animals, suggesting that this vividly painted imagery may have been a vital means of early communication. The exit from the cave leads to another exhibit: a re-created print shop from the time of Gutenberg. Using a sturdy printing press, complete with type, ink and lots of paper, children work their way through successive steps in the printing process. "In an age of media manipulation," says Ann Lewin, "even this utterly simple series of actions can be a liberating experience. It says to the child, 'I can do it. I can also create a message.' "

Some of the most absorbing experiences occur in the museum's video animation lab, which is decorated with original drawings by Chuck Jones. "To animate means to 'invoke life,' " says Jones, and by using an animation camera and videotape, a child can bring her drawings to life in a few minutes. And, beyond the delight at discovering the secret laws of motion, a child can also begin to grasp the meaning and importance of "process." (Having spent half an hour to produce a flicker of movement in her animated story of a bicycle race, a girl turns to her friend and sighs, "Imagine how long it takes to make something like *Cinderella* . . . Whew!") One of Ann Lewin's goals is to awaken in the child an appreciation of the fact that all of life is a process. "The patience and ability to work through a long series of steps—to figure things out—is a foundation for the child's creative life later on," says Lewin.

Creative work later in life often requires that we solve problems as members of a team. The purely intellectual challenges of finding solutions become increasingly intermixed with the emotional demands of collaboration and competition.

© 1991 WARNER BROS. INC., LJE INC.

The Creative Spirit

Odyssey of the Mind

Sam Micklus loves Fazio's Building Supply, a seemingly endless warehouse in New Jersey. At Fazio's you can find just about anything. "There should be a sign outside that says, 'IF WE DON'T HAVE IT, YOU DON'T NEED IT,'" says Micklus as he prowls through its corridors. Micklus is on a mission. He's looking for odd combinations of things that he can use to pose creative challenges to youngsters.

Sam's search for quirky objects is part of Odyssey of the Mind, a program designed to encourage creative problem-solving. As founder of Odyssey, Micklus poses perplexing challenges to students who work together in teams in an international competition. It is a creativity contest; entries are judged for their ingenuity more than their elegance. There's no right answer, just the most imaginative. It's a sort of kids' Olympics for innovation. In 1990, more than one million students around the world participated.

"There is no spoon-fed, cookbook way of solving the problems posed by Odyssey of the Mind. Everybody has his own way of solving them," says Micklus.

"In my opinion a great group of problem-solvers are farm kids. They're used to watching their parents improvise when something goes wrong. If they have a two thousand–pound bull to get on a truck and it doesn't want to go, what do they do? They don't call in a bull mover. They figure out a way to do it."

At the Odyssey of the Mind competition: an Olympics for innovation.

Working in teams is essential to the Odyssey challenge. "In today's world very few people do something creative all by themselves," comments Micklus. "Almost everything we have to do is a team effort. They have to work together, depend on each other, negotiate with each other. That's a tremendous lifelong skill." The teams that do the best, Micklus says, are those that brainstorm together, generating dozens of creative solutions before they decide which one to pursue.

BEYOND RIGHT OR WRONG

BELIEVE FIRMLY that creativity can be taught," says Micklus. "Creative thinking is a skill and can be honed like any other." He adds, however, that one way to snuff out creativity is to pose right/wrong questions and penalize children for wrong answers. The Odyssey's antidote: open-ended questions, limited only by the boundaries of the imagination.

"If we offer questions or problems to young people that have open-ended solutions to them, we're way ahead," says Micklus. "Rather than telling them, this is how you do it, we take the opposite view: here's the problem, you figure it out. If someone asks us a question, we answer it with another question."

One year, for example, students were challenged to create a kind of robotic being, a character with a face that could show emotions. And beyond that, the idea was to have this character laugh and cry as part of an original comedy routine.

Another challenge was to design, build, and drive a vehicle propelled by a rowing motion, use the vehicle in a race, and find an imaginative way to visually and dramatically represent three countries the vehicle might have visited.

Inventive fun: a vehicle propelled by a rowing motion.

A classic Odyssey problem is to have a team assemble a balsa-wood-and-glue structure from parts they've made. The structure must balance itself and hold as much weight as possible. They have fifteen minutes to assemble it from their team-made prefabricated parts.

One of the most basic ideas is to get kids to "break set" by using an ordinary object in an extraordinary way. For instance, Micklus says of a hydraulic jack: "It took me years to think of a way to use it in a challenge. But when the piston in the jack rises, you have an enormous amount of power. So we challenged kids to build a vehicle that would be powered by the piston rising on a jack."

Problems like this demand thoughtful inventiveness. For instance, here's one way to use the jack to power a vehicle: think of a long beam balanced on a leverage point, like a teeter totter. If the jack were positioned under the beam near an end that was anchored to the ground, then the longer end would rise as the jack raised. And because of the piston's power, that beam could pull a rope as it lifted, which in turn could turn an axle . . .

Of course, you probably thought of that already.

NOTHING LESS THAN "GREAT"

THE COMPETITIVE NATURE of the Odyssey program adds an edge to the creative spirit. The competition does not pit children against one another; rather, it gets them working side by side, blending the creative act with a drive for excellence.

There is a role for competition once you've mastered an area; it increases the challenge. As Micklus sees it: "If we give a student a project to do, we tend to say, 'Well, this is good enough,' even if we know it isn't quite right. But if they're competing, kids say, 'Well, if this isn't just right, let's make it right. Let's pay attention to detail. Let's make this thing as good as we possibly can.' " That pursuit of excellence is an element that the competitive nature of Odyssey adds to the creative caldron.

"Part of sparking creativity is getting kids to wake up in the morning and be really excited about what they are going to do. If they won't settle for something that is just okay, but want to have something that is great, they will have learned a lifelong lesson that will help them really make a contribution. When people will go that one step beyond, give that one hundred and ten percent, that is what separates a good society from a great one."

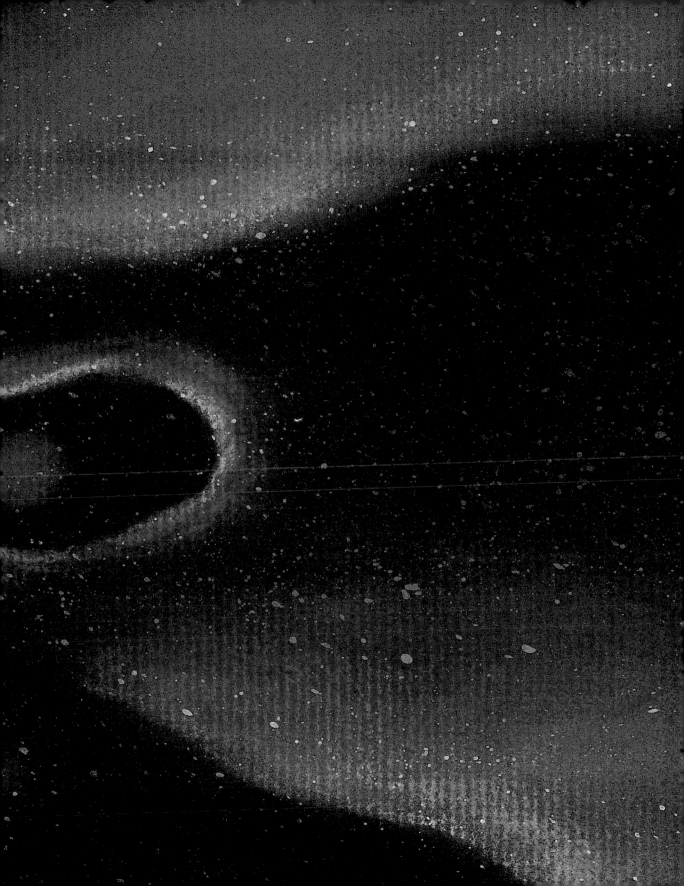

CHAPTER THREE

Creativity AT WORK

"The world of making and fetching and carrying and buying and selling to which you give the greater part of your waking life is ruled by certain laws, obsessed by certain defects (which perhaps you may help to cure), and threatened by certain dangers you may help to avert."

–H. G. Wells

MOVIE STAR NEWS

THE CLASSIC Broadway musical *How to Succeed in Business Without Really Trying* satirized the traditional way of playing the business game. In one song, the perennial mail room clerk explains to the ambitious newcomer, J. Pierpont Finch, how to rise in the corporate world.

The clerk says that when *he* joined the firm as a brash young man, he told himself, "Don't get any ideas." And he hasn't had one in years, he assures Finch with pride. He played it safe, "the company way." What's his point of view? He has no point of view. Whatever the company thinks . . . he thinks so, too. By playing it the company way, our clerk admits, he will never rise to the top. But by never taking a risk, he'll be sure to be around year after year.

How to Succeed roasted the conformity and inbred fear of innovation of the past. But times have changed—or have they? Here are the candid observations of a contemporary executive with twenty-one years of experience as a top manager with a multinational firm:

> The company of today must change profoundly...much of our employees' energy goes into repression, hiding the truth, concealing problems, refusing to face reality....This feeling of being boxed in is exacerbated by the proclamation to

Play it safe—sage advice to a newcomer in the movie version of **How to Succeed in Business Without Really Trying.**

managers: "If *you* can't do it, I'll find someone who can." Inside most corporations there is little tolerance for insubordination or public criticism. People see the lies and abuses, the destruction of those among them who dare to be bold, iconoclastic, and creative. They sense the lack of trust, the fear that is palpable in the corridors and offices. They manifest the pathology of "groupthink" in meetings, where silence greets the manager's call for problems or differing viewpoints. Employees in corporate America today live in terror of being seen as wrong, of making a mistake, of being busted or neutralized. Those with the temerity to speak truth to power usually suffer for it, and the net result is to leave the corporation stuck in the morass of the party line.

These are strong words, yet businesses increasingly need workers who are independent-minded, who are willing to take the risk of speaking out, who feel free to respond imaginatively to change—who are, in a word, creative. Creativity requires the corporate culture to encourage more open and much safer expression of what may sometimes be irritating or unsettling new ideas. It requires that people be knit together in collaborative teams.

The question is: How does a company go from being a place where people are afraid to take risks and don't really trust one another, to a place where it's safe to propose new ideas? This question has taken on a new urgency because the workplace and the nature of work itself have undergone dramatic changes. More and more companies depend for their survival on their ability to respond quickly to shifting consumer demands for new products and services. Businesses now compete in a global marketplace, in which competitors are committed to continued innovation.

Individual companies that fail to respond flexibly to change are almost certainly doomed to fail. But much more is at stake. The economies of entire nations depend upon the emerging creative capacities of their people. As never before, the overall quality of a nation's life hinges on the application of intelligence, even wisdom, to the solution of problems at work.

Reforming the Workplace

FROM MACHINE TO ORGANISM

THE NEED FOR creativity is changing how the workplace is organized and what people do. These changes center on the use and interpretation of information: the basis for ideas. A company's future depends upon how well it acquires, interprets, and acts upon information. For instance, Detroit's failure in the 1970s to properly understand and act upon the American driver's desire for fuel-efficient cars allowed Japanese automakers to make huge inroads into the American auto market.

Today the spread of information technologies—including computers and databases—throughout the workplace is bringing about a sea change in the business world. As Harvard Business School's Shoshona Zuboff observes, companies are attempting to use these technologies to collect data about their own operations in a process of continual learning and self-improvement. These new streams of information *should* allow companies to constantly refine their products and services, and to upgrade their production, distribution, or marketing. But, as Zuboff says, "smart machines demand smart workers."

Elaborate new technologies are not enough. By themselves, they are like a brilliantly engineered car with no driver or destination. The entire process of gathering and using information is ultimately shaped by workers who are "smart" in the broadest sense: who have fresh perceptions and are willing to ask penetrating questions.

How workers interpret information—how they make sense of it and decide what it means—is as important as the information itself. Interpre-

Creativity at Work

tation is, in fact, a creative act. But the degree of creativity is influenced by our feelings, including those on the fringes of our awareness. Our belief that we can speak out without fear of retribution, our feeling of being trusted by others, a confidence in our own intuition—all these affect how we respond to the information before us. We need only remind ourselves of the many painful instances, such as the *Challenger* disaster, when presumably rational executives were—despite adequate information—simply unwilling or unable to take action.

Since creativity draws upon a person's facts *and* values, upon what is conscious and unconscious, analytic and intuitive, a creative work environment truly requires the enthusiasm and commitment of the whole person. For example, at Stanford University's Graduate School of Business a course on creativity has as its theme: *Who am I? What is my work?* The student is asked to reflect on her true potential—that which gives life meaning, satisfaction, and a driving sense of purpose.

There are many ways in which the creative spirit can find expression in the workplace. The creation of new products is the most obvious, but there are other ways, such as providing better services to customers, innovations in management, improvements in distribution methods, or new ideas for financing the business. Creative ideas can also be used to strengthen the organization itself by, for example, increasing the initiative of workers. One such innovation is the elimination of restrictive and bureaucratic job descriptions that put workers in "boxes" and limit their performance. Another idea (used successfully by a Swedish manufacturing company as well as others in Brazil and the United States) is to share all financial information—such as the weekly cash flow—with all of the employees. Elimination of traditional corporate secrets helps workers to understand the larger reality of the business and encourages them to generate ideas of their own that reduce costs and increase revenues.

Changes that bring about a better workplace are the result of the combined efforts of both managers and workers. Innovative business leaders can create a climate that empowers workers; at the same time employees can request work assignments that draw upon their unique capacities. When both managers and workers adopt a creative outlook, a subtle but powerful change begins to occur in the workplace. A premium is placed on the *process* of work, not simply the end product. Value is placed on how workers can learn new things, develop personally, and express their insights. The organization is viewed less as a kind of huge impersonal machine and more like a complex living organism guided by a lively intelligence that needs to be continually stimulated.

WHAT WE CAN DO

SINCE CREATIVE PROBLEM-SOLVING requires the psychological commitment of the whole person, the modern workplace must undergo vital changes. From the efforts of pioneering companies around the world, a set of key ideas are emerging that can change the psychology of the workplace.

Beyond Hierarchy

ONE IDEA IS to reduce the negative effects of hierarchy, to "flatten" the corporate pyramid. Businesses are more productive when those at the front lines—in contact with customers—have more responsibility and access to a wider range of information about the whole organization. Employees are allowed to use this information, along with their intuition, to make critical decisions on the spot. A cardinal virtue becomes trust in what people can do, not blind adherence to the "company way."

A Safe Haven for Ideas

THIS MEANS a willingness to let ideas emerge freely and to be receptive to them. It means curbing cynicism and harsh judgments, so that employees feel free to make iconoclastic suggestions and even to ask what appear to be "dumb questions." It requires valuing intuitive as well as analytic approaches to problem-solving, recognizing that emotions and subjective values play a key role in generating new ideas. This demands an atmosphere of respect, an environment where people have the security to share their inspirations with others.

The Man Who Hated His Boss But Loved His Job

Those of us who find ourselves working in less than enlightened circumstances can take heart from this fable of the modern workplace.

① *Once upon a time there was a man who loved his job and his fellow workers. And he made a pretty good living.*

② *But there was one thing wrong—his boss.*

③ *In fact, his boss made his life so miserable that there was only one thing the man could do: he decided to quit.*

The Creative Spirit

4 *So he went to a headhunter to find himself a new job. But he remained very unhappy because really he wanted to stay where he was.*

5 *At the peak of his desperation the man had a creative breatkthrough. Why hadn't he thought of it before? He went back to the headhunter and gave his boss's name and résumé to the headhunter.*

6 *The headhunter found his boss a better job, which the boss happily took.*

7 *Meanwhile the man remained at his job and was eventually promoted to what had been his boss's position.*

More Than Just a Job

A THIRD KEY IDEA is to expand the very meaning of work. Within the company itself, the workplace can become a more homelike and humane setting, including amenities such as day care. It can be a physical environment that enlivens the senses, promotes spontaneous interaction among people in different jobs and at different levels, and allows moments for mental relaxation during the workday.

The meaning of work can also change when the company adopts a broader role in the community. By responding to social needs in the community, and by acknowledging that it not only creates wealth but also influences the quality of people's lives, a company can make work "more than just a job." As one executive put it: "It becomes a *movement* rather than just a business."

PIONEERING WOMEN AND MEN

THESE ARE more than appealing but impractical ideas. They are actually working for business today. In this chapter we'll see how some pioneering companies—and the women and men who run them—have put these principles into action. Among the places and people we'll encounter:

Anita Roddick, president of The Body Shop International.

❀ British Business Woman of the Year **Anita Roddick**, founder and president of the Body Shop International.

An unorthodox business from the start, the Body Shop sells its own line of natural cosmetics. Its products are based on traditional beauty aids, many inspired by Third World cultures, and are developed without animal testing. And the windows of the Body Shop feature posters promoting ecological awareness rather than pictures of perfectly made-up models.

When Roddick started out, she recalls, "We were naive about how businesses are usually run. We didn't know that you could take liberties with the truth. For instance, most companies didn't put any henna in their 'henna shampoo'—they just put in a perfume that they thought smelled of henna. So we brought out a henna shampoo that was jammed with the real thing. Unfortunately, henna smells like horse manure. But we felt we had to be honest, so we said, "Don't worry if it smells a bit like horse manure—that's henna."

To the mainstream of the cosmetics industry, the Body Shop's approach seemed almost ludicrous, its chances of survival slim. Today the Body Shop has more than five hundred outlets in close to forty countries, and a fifty percent annual growth rate. And now the major cosmetics companies are following Roddick's lead, adding their own lines of natural cosmetics.

At the Body Shop, creativity is primed through constant change. Says Roddick, "Creativity comes by breaking the rules, by saying you're in love with the anarchist." As a manager, her attitude is that "you have to be constantly open to suggestions and you don't have a rhetoric that says you'll listen and then do nothing."

Roddick believes that "a company can be run in a moral way—make money but enhance the spirituality of the workplace. Bringing spirituality into the workplace is very much like saying, 'Why should how I act in my workplace be any different from how I interact with my family at home?' It's making sure the company runs on feminine principles where the major ethic is *care*."

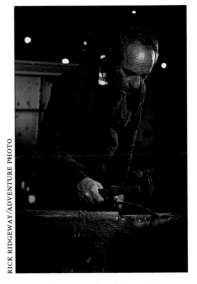

Yvon Chouinard at his anvil.

❋ **Yvon Chouinard** did not set out to found one of the most innovative sportswear companies in the world. Not at all. His company, Patagonia, in southern California, was spawned by his passion for mountain climbing and his need for a good piton, the sharp spike climbers hammer into cliff sides.

"There I was, interested in climbing, and there were no good tools available," Chouinard recalls. "So when I was eighteen I decided to go out and buy a little coal-fired forge and an anvil, some hammers and tongs, to make my own pitons. I tried to improve on the only ones we could buy at that time, ones from Europe. They were made of soft steel, and you could only use them once. So I decided to try to make them out of a much better quality steel.

"I made a few for myself, and then for friends, and then pretty soon I was selling them. So that's it. It isn't that we invented this climbing equipment, but we did a lot of innovation."

Indeed, says Chouinard, the business snuck up on him: "It got to the point where I couldn't make just a few of these every day and call it a business. I had to make more and more, and now we have five hundred people working here." In 1990, Patagonia had revenues of $120 million and an annual growth rate of thirty percent.

The price of that success, says Chouinard, is that "I've become a paper shuffler. But to clear my mind once in a while, I keep the blacksmith's shop here and work away. Because this is what I really enjoy."

The casual way Chouinard got into business is completely in character, and is reflected in an unorthodox management style. "I had become a businessman whether I wanted to admit it or not, but I decided that if I was going to stick with it, I was going to do it on my own terms," he says. "Doing it on my own terms means breaking the rules."

One of the rules Chouinard breaks is in his decision not to compete head-on with other companies in his industry. "We try to make products that are non-competitive," Chouinard says. "I don't want to make the same product as another company. Then I'd have to compete head-on with quality, price, distribution, advertising—all the normal ways of selling whenever you have a product that's identical to someone else's.

A worker at Skaltek, where everyone has the same job title.

"Instead of doing that, I'd rather put my money and energy into having a very strong R&D department. Then we can come out with unique products and there's no competition. We run with those products as fast as we can, sell as many as we can, until everybody copies us. Then we just drop the product and go on in a completely different direction. We try to do things differently from what the business books tell you."

✺ Imagine a company without a hierarchy. A company where power is dispersed instead of focused at the top of the pyramid. Where there are no financial secrets, and every worker can know the company's weekly cash flow. Where everyone shares responsibility. Where personal growth and independent initiative is encouraged, because it enhances the whole. A utopian dream?

Not at all. It exists in Stockholm, Sweden.

The Creative Spirit

Skaltek designs, manufactures, and sells heavy machinery used by the wire and cable industry. Skaltek's custom-built machines are sold all over the world, and the company's success is due in part to the unusual way it supports the creativity of its workers.

Skaltek's founder, Öystein Skalleberg, was an engineer who had worked far too many years in traditional firms and disliked how they were run. He couldn't stand the competition, the artificial distance between people, and the distrust. He found company secrets and withholding of information from employees distasteful. He couldn't participate in the "defend my box in the hierarchy" corporate mentality.

So Skalleberg left his old firm with the vision of starting *his* kind of company. At Skaltek, no one has a title that confers some privileged status; everyone has one and the same title. There are no cookie-cutter job descriptions, and the workers who build a machine at Skaltek may be the same ones who sell it to the customer. This way, information about the use of the machines can be fed directly back into ideas for improving the machines.

Taking risks at the Pecos Learning Center.

Perhaps more radical, there's a weekly meeting of all employees, where there's a full report of the previous week's cash flow: sales, expenses . . . everything. Full disclosure. And because everyone knows all the facts about where the money comes from and goes, salaries are set openly and are subject to discussion by everybody.

❋ There are other ways of changing the psychology of the workplace so that employees feel confident enough to freely express their ideas. One of the most unusual approaches is taken by an outdoor, adventure/learning course held for employees of the Midwest Energy Company in Sioux City, Iowa. The program, called "Playing to Win," is conducted by the **Pecos River Learning Center** of Santa Fe, New Mexico. The course is a rite of passage designed to teach people—including bosses—that it's okay to take risks, change the routine, even to look scared in front of your colleagues. The idea is that there's no punishment for taking a leap.

During the program, Midwest Energy workers, who know each other mainly through their day-to-day routines and roles, encounter each other with a new immediacy and even vulnerability. In a sense it is like meeting each other for the first time because of the physical and emotional challenges they face together. For example, the Corporate Tower is a vertical struggle up a fifty-foot wall studded with pegs. Co-workers are attached to each other by bungee cords, so that they must coordinate their climb, assisting one another.

Events like this one offer an opportunity for personal growth and team effort. As employees confront each of these challenges—and most people find them somewhat daunting—the support of their workmates gives them the courage to go through with it. As a manager stands poised to let himself down a Zip Line from a platform dizzyingly high above the ground, it is a literal and figurative first step.

The chief executive officer of the Pecos River Learning Center, Larry Wilson, makes the point that "most people find a lot of situations in their lives where they just aren't willing to take that first step. But if they are willing to take that first step, everything good follows."

© 1991 WARNER BROS. INC., LJE INC.

Beyond Hierarchy

THE NEED FOR HIERARCHY is, for the most part, an unquestioned assumption in the business world. As Anita Roddick observes, "Business is an institution that is deeply conservative. In England, it's run on the principles of hierarchy, much like the military. God help you if you park your car in the managing director's space."

While success in a hierarchy has its privileges, it can also exact a terrible price. Along with a top position comes the fear of losing that position. To protect himself, a hierarchical manager will often seek to eliminate threats by controlling the flow of information. Disturbing or disappointing information is suppressed. The inflated body-counts and calculatedly optimistic "light at the end of the tunnel" forecasts by those managing the Vietnam War are good examples of hierarchy run amok.

Climbing the hierarchical ladder can mean keeping potential rivals in the dark, even if those rivals are co-workers with important contributions to make within the firm. It can mean devaluing or discounting information that doesn't confirm expectations or meet predetermined goals. The destruction of the *Challenger* may have been due, in no small measure, to management's unwillingness to give full credit to disturbing engineering information about faulty O-rings.

Traditionally, the allure of a hierarchical system has been that it permits those at the top to transmit instructions to large numbers of people, with little or no fear of contradiction. The ancient model for this was kingship, with its core assumption that all wisdom and knowledge emanated from a divinely inspired authority. As history shows, one result of this conceit was that hierarchical systems were shot through with deception and often murderous unrest as people struggled behind the scenes for power. Although the hoary tradition of unquestioned authority—once exemplified by the priesthood and the military—has never completely disappeared from business, it has clearly lost its usefulness.

One reason is that managers today rely not so much on instruction as information. Jan Carlzon, president and CEO of Scandinavian Airlines System (SAS), explains that information is the opposite of instruction. "Instruction tells you what you're not allowed to do, what your limits are," he says. "But information tells you about your possibilities. A person who has sound information cannot escape taking responsibility."

The style of management in which information is hoarded at the top and decisions flow only from the top down leads to work done mechanically, without inspiration. Jan Carlzon says, "We controlled people at work by giving orders and instructions, telling them down to every detail what they should do out there—although we never had any real feeling for or information about what the customer really wanted. The worst of it was that the instructions really amounted to telling people what they were not allowed to do; it was just a way of limiting their responsibility.

"But what you need to do today is open things up so people can take responsibility," Carlzon adds. "You have to give them the authority they need to make decisions on the spot. You do that by telling people where you want to get to as a company, and the strategy you want to use to get there. Then you give the people the freedom within the limits of your business strategy to act on behalf of the company."

⟲

JOB TITLE: LEONARDO DA VINCI

ONE OF THE WAYS people at Skaltek take responsibility is by signing their work. Every machine that goes out the door bears the signatures of the designer, the engineer, and the other key workers who made it. That insignia serves as a personal link to the customer.

Signing their work means that everyone at Skaltek is treated, literally, like an artist. "Every human being is a Leonardo da Vinci," says company founder Öystein Skalleberg. "The only problem is that he doesn't know it. His parents didn't know it, and they didn't treat him like a Leonardo. Therefore he didn't become like a Leonardo. That's my basic theory."

That philosophy has led to the unique corporate culture that sets Skaltek apart. For example, take the matter of titles and business cards. At Skaltek, everyone has the identical business card: a photo of the person, his name and phone number, and the title: "Responsible Person." Says Skalleberg, "I don't believe in titles, because the moment you have a title, you put the person in a box and make a declaration defining what the person is. If we had a title, what should it be? 'Leonardo da Vinci' or 'Unlimited Possibilities' or something like that."

But there is a more concrete way people define themselves at Skaltek. "The products display who they are. The product is a result of the people themselves—their thoughts, their ambitions, their needs, their striving for quality. We have no quality control," Skalleberg says. "It's all built on individual responsibility. You could say we have one quality controller per person—and he works twenty-four hours per day, for free."

Skaltek machines bear the signatures of those who made them.

The fundamental idea is that, once given responsibility, a worker begins to develop a moral conscience about his work. That sense of responsibility is enhanced by the fact that many who design and build the machines at Skaltek also accompany those machines when they are delivered, showing their customers how to operate them. As a result, Skaltek workers create a personal bond with their customers.

If people have responsibility for how they do their jobs, then they are free to find imaginative solutions to problems posed to them. At Patagonia, says Yvon Chouinard, "The role of management is to instigate change, to throw down the gauntlet and say, 'This is the standard that we're going to set.' "

For example, at Patagonia the decision was made to forgo the button machines used throughout the clothing industry to sew on buttons. The reason? The stitches came undone too easily. So a standard was set: no Patagonia button would ever come off, no matter what.

"We just threw the glove down and made the challenge," says Chouinard. "So then everybody in the company has to figure out how to do it. It forces people to be imaginative and to adapt. And it also makes for an excellent product."

Absence of Judgment

THE BIGGEST block to living a creative life is the voice of blame and criticism within each of us: the voice of judgment, or the VOJ for short. A good way to start dealing with it is to acknowledge that you have it! Take a moment to recall a time when you had an idea and were hesitant or afraid to verbalize or act on it. Perhaps later somebody else did the very thing you had been thinking of, and you felt despondent about not having acted on your idea in the first place. The VOJ is that part of you that makes you both afraid to do something and depressed after you didn't do it.

The VOJ assumes different forms. The voice inside of you is usually the most daunting—but there is also judgment by others, including cultural judgments such as the rules of etiquette that discourage "unconventional" social behavior. Once it gets hold of you, the VOJ can lead you into a maze of negativity, including the following absurd situation. The VOJ inhibits you from doing something. Your VOJ then makes you feel depressed about your weakness of will. Next, your VOJ condemns you harshly for being depressed (it's not part of your self-image). Then, a friend comes along and chides you for both not following through on your idea and for being depressed!

✳◎✳
OWNING THE RESULTS

WHEN SARAH NOLAN was made president of Amex Life Assurance, she inherited a company that was responding sluggishly to customer needs. There was a rigid hierarchy of workers, with little communication between people doing different tasks, and even less between levels in the hierarchy.

When she came from New York to the company headquarters in San Rafael, California, executives there told her the problems were intractable—that was just the way things were done in the insurance industry. But Nolan asked five managers from various parts of the business to set up an office in an unoccupied business park away from the main building. Faced with an empty office and a charge from their president to make radical changes, they set about reinventing one division of the organization.

As one of the five, a director of customer service, put it, "Under the old traditional way of running a business, I was totally isolated; I had a big office and people came to see me by appointment." Those inefficiencies of the hierarchy were eliminated in a series of drastic changes:

❂ The managers designed an open office without floor to ceiling walls, unlike the rigidly divided offices typical in the insurance industry.

❂ The levels of hierarchy were cut from ten to three.

❂ With a computer on every desk, everyone had access to and could use all necessary information, including that which had formerly been reserved for top management.

❂ Innovative ideas were welcomed.

❂ Rigid job distinctions were erased, creating an environment where people were given expanded responsibility; everybody was prepared to do every task.

The result: the company was able to be far more responsive to customer needs than ever before. The time it took to process applications and deal with customer problems plummeted. And profits for the division increased 700 percent. "It's staggering," says Nolan, "how far people will go if they own the results."

One way of getting employees to "own the results" of their work is to make them aware of the true financial status of the company. At Skaltek, for example, there are no financial secrets. Letting people know all the facts has the effect of involving them in everything. Skalleberg sees this as a major benefit: "If you really want to have cooperation and teamwork, you have to involve people not just in a part of things, but in the whole thing."

One way this is done at Skaltek is the Monday morning meeting that is called "Information Cash Flow." There everyone learns the company's exact flow of money for the week, how many orders came in—all the details that are usually reserved for a privileged few in the upper echelons of management.

"We do about 100 million kronen turnover each week, and we have been up to 25 million in net cash—and it's never been a secret," says Skalleberg. "All the people know. They say at other companies that if you tell people this kind of information, they will jump up and ask you for a higher salary. But that's not true, not at all. They are proud of how well we do. But they see after a few months that this week's 25 million drops to 12, or 10. And then they start to understand what business really is."

Says one Skaltek worker: "We know what the machine we sell costs us and how much money we will make in a sale. And then we know all the other costs, like salaries and travel, taxes and depreciation." A better sense of what things actually cost, and what each person is producing, gives workers at Skaltek a more realistic idea of what people should be paid. "I find it quite natural to know it all," adds the worker. "If you just work in the dark, you really don't know what *you* contribute." Another worker says, "My salary has been set openly by the whole team. Everybody has an opinion about my salary. And it feels good."

Notes Skalleberg, "Nobody here knows who will set their salary next year, because we involve everyone in it." And he adds wryly, "Therefore they have to smile in all directions and try to serve everyone."

In most people the creative spirit and the VOJ continually wage a pitched battle. Even before your ideas reach conscious awareness, let alone fruition, the VOJ can cut them down with a fusillade of negative messages.

"Who do you think you are?" POW!

Usually that is enough to kill your fledgling idea, but if it isn't, the VOJ can continue the attack until the idea is dead:

"Admit it, you're pretty shaky in your job."

"They'll think you're crazy."

"You'll look like a jerk."

"Sure it's a good idea, but *you'll* never be able to present it."

"Remember, your father and mother never amounted to anything."

"If you fail on this one, you'll never have another chance."

"Better keep quiet and let someone else do it."

This mental warfare goes on throughout the day, affecting mundane interactions that may, paradoxically, be crucial to your well-being.

For instance, say you have an urge to say hello to someone you see at work or in a restaurant. At the critical moment the VOJ attacks: "Can't you see that she is talking to someone else? You're not important enough to interrupt them." The impulse to make the contact is crushed. Who knows where that contact might have led?

The VOJ is usually instilled in childhood, when our parents, teachers, and other authority figures try to tell us the right way to behave, peppering their good advice and exhortations with words like *stupid, fool, jerk,* and perhaps more important, using a tone of voice and a look that can have a lasting emotional impact on a child. This VOJ is internalized and we carry it with us for the rest of our lives.

Now, you might say, "That VOJ you're condemning is what tells me the right thing to do. Without it I might have made a lot of mistakes in my life." This is an example of your VOJ trying to get off the hook by clouding the distinction between thoughts that are inhibiting (the VOJ) and thoughts that are enabling, that help us to move forward.

Both voices offer critical assessments of things, but the spirit in which they speak is radically different. One is rooted in fear and holds us back. The other is based on curiosity and the desire to better ourselves. It allows us to pursue our goals intelligently.

GO TO PAGE 124

SMALL IS BETTER

SIZE AFFECTS creativity in the workplace. Bigness by its very nature appears antithetical to the effective expression of an individual's ideas. The best environment for creative work seems to be on the scale of the extended family, where people can get to know each other.

This suggests that large, monolithic corporations be broken into smaller, semi-autonomous units. An advocate of this approach is Jim Collins, a lecturer at Stanford University's Graduate School of Business. "As our society has evolved from small organizations to large ones," says Collins, "it has stifled innovation. We used to have small local schools; now we have large school systems. We used to have family physicians; now we have immense bureaucratized medical centers. We used to have town meetings where you heard everyone's voice; now we have huge elections where many people don't turn out to vote. Everything is oversized.

"Of course, there are economies in doing things on a mass scale. But you lose one thing: that creative edge. Massiveness breeds conformity."

The history of economic growth in the West shows that its prosperity is largely based on a succession of innovative leaps forward. These leaps—the invention of a completely new technology, product, or service—have tended to come from small entrepreneurial firms or semi-independent divisions of corporations.

This argues, says Collins, that we need to consider the benefits of slicing organizations into smaller and smaller units, finding an autonomy within a larger whole. "Silicon Valley," says Collins, "is a place where small companies, and small parts of big companies, have been able to strike out on their own without being stifled by big bureaucracies. There have been spin-offs of spin-offs of spin-offs, each conceived by a daring group of visionaries. It's been like taking a big diamond and cutting it into smaller ones, then having each grow back into big diamonds again."

JAZZ AS A MODEL FOR WORK

There are few creative teams more closely knit than a jazz ensemble in the heat of creation. Each musician is on his own, and yet they are creating a single weave of sound. Jazz is a good model for creative work in small groups.

Benny Golson, jazz musician and composer of the music for *The Creative Spirit* television series, describes how musicians work together: "First of all, collaboration is a matter of choice. But once the choice is made, it is made because those two or three or more people who are collaborating believe in one another.

"But then once you do, it is very much like iron sharpening iron. When you rub two pieces together they refine each other. You tend to fill in the gaps that the other didn't consider. One person becomes a barometer for the other. And one person encourages the other.

Mutual trust is what lets a jazz ensemble take off: "You are going into another zone now, and you are not going alone. You are going with other people, and the purpose is to create. And that can be exciting—as long as you believe in one another."

CLIMBING TOGETHER

A CLOSE-KNIT TEAM, drawing on the particular strengths and skills of each member of the group, may be smarter and more effective than any individual member of that group. Yale psychologist Robert Sternberg calls it a "group IQ"—the sum total or even the product of all the talents of each person in the group. What one person lacks can be made up by another member of the team; any member's brilliance is shared by all. When a team is harmonious, the group IQ is highest. That places a premium on a leader who can create a smoothly working team: a leader who knows the virtues of sharing, trust, and encouragement.

Innovation requires two broad strokes: the creation of a new idea and its implementation. Although a lone inventor may come up with a breakthrough idea, it is increasingly difficult to carry it to fruition in the marketplace without assembling a support team. And more and more often the great breakthroughs come from the efforts of a team. The next generation of super-computers, of genetically engineered medicines, of renewable energy sources, will likely spring from collaborative efforts.

The value of collaboration comes more naturally in cultures like Japan, where group harmony is a cardinal value. It is a harder lesson to learn in cultures like that of the U.S., where the trail-blazing lone hero has long been idolized, and where the goals of the individual are so often placed before those of the group. But even those used to working alone can learn the advantages of teamwork.

Building a cooperative spirit at Pecos River.

One way to awaken people to the benefits of teamwork is the Corporate Tower event at the Pecos River Learning Center, where the employees of Midwest Energy went through a training course. The Tower is a simulated rock climb, a sheer fifty-foot wall combed with small pegs. Three people attack the Tower at once, all tied together with bungee cords—an action metaphor for creative cooperation. The event is a concrete demonstration of the maxim: "I have to do it myself, and I can't do it alone."

The reason: each person climbing can't go faster or farther than the other two people he or she is hooked to. "As you get higher and higher on the Tower it gets pretty exciting," says Larry Wilson of the Center. "You really need to support each other, to encourage each other, to reach down and help someone. And you need to be willing to ask for help, which for some of our macho males is tough to do.

"But when they get in this predicament, they find themselves asking for help and getting it, and find they do better when they get that help. It welds a team—three people under real stress and pressure performing at a much higher level than they expected they would ever be able to."

◎* THE LEADER AS PROVOCATEUR

HOW DO YOU KEEP a young, enthusiastic group of workers on their creative toes? Anita Roddick has some unusual ideas.

"You have to have the ability to surprise them," says Roddick. "I'll go into a meeting with my staff when I visit them around the world, and I'll sit down and ask them, 'What really ticks you off about us?'

"At first, of course, their thought is, Is she really saying those words?

Is she daring to suggest that the company does things wrong and screws things up? "You have to break down their notions of you being a big businesswoman or a giant company that is successful. When you break through the barriers those models create, you can get to the questions that really matter: What do you feel about your work? What do you love about it? How can I make your job more exciting?

"The only role left for me in this company is to motivate and challenge, to open up new avenues, new ways you can create an experience for feeling alive. Selling moisture cream, I guarantee, does not make anybody feel alive.

"But they're going to love their ability to break the rules and be mischievous in the work environment, because they've been conditioned by our society not to challenge anything. So we just give them opportunities for that challenge.

"For example, when we did our recycling campaign, we printed 28 million bags for Body Shop products. Simple paper bags, all recycled. And we asked the government, Why aren't you printing telephone bills and gas bills and electricity bills on recycled paper? We put the idea on posters in our stores; we told the consumer how many millions we'd save each year, how many trees we'd save. And just to be cheeky— and this is an example of creativity at work—

Creating new products at the Body Shop.

we also put the phone number or the address of the administrator to contact. They were bombarded with complaints! You just have to show people how they can do it, and it puts their thinking on another plane."

"You have to give people the freedom to play and take risks. For example, Friday afternoon all our research and development labs are closed, but anyone who wants to play around making products can go in. And if they come up with a brilliant product, we'll pursue it, market it, and give them royalties. That's opening things up."

This new style of leadership, which gives employees the permission and the protection to tap their creative potential, is absolutely essential in

Heuristic:

Say Hello and Then Good-bye to Your VOJ

YOU HAVE opportunities all day long to practice defeating the VOJ.

In the spirit of "know thine enemy," start by becoming aware of how your VOJ operates. Try to understand where it comes from. How often does it come up during a day? Here's an exercise you can do.

✎ Think of a person with whom you have an intimate relationship or work very closely. Take a piece of paper and write at the top: "The trouble with (name) is" and list major criticisms you have of that person, e.g., "Doesn't follow through on assignments" or "Always expects to be the center of attention." Next, on a sheet headed "The trouble with me is..." make a parallel list about yourself.

Now compare the two lists. Do your criticisms of yourself echo your criticisms of the other person? If to an extent they do, this is not surprising. Psychologists have long been familiar with a phenomenon called projection. Essentially, projection means attributing to others qualities that, for various reasons, we are reluctant to recognize in ourselves.

The lists can be used to help you realize not only how the VOJ works against you but also how it intrudes into your relationships with others.

GO TO PAGE 127 ↝

business today. It is a recognition that an original turn of mind on the part of just one worker can give an organization a competitive advantage.

It was just a decade or two ago that in many countries and industries around the globe the demand for products and services was greater than the output. That allowed some managers the luxury of steering a company from central headquarters as they wanted, and left customers having to accept what they got. But today global competition, practically without regard for borders, has put the customer in the driver's seat as never before. A company that wants to compete is compelled to listen to the market and detect customers' preferences. The competitive advantage lies in an imaginative response at the frontier where the company meets the customer.

"The moment of truth is whenever you deal with customers," says Jan Carlzon of SAS. "If you leave them satisfied, then the company is in good shape. But if those moments are handled in a bad way, you leave a trail of dissatisfied customers, and eventually a business that fails." He adds, however, that the imaginative response can't be made from the distance of central headquarters: "It's out there on the front lines, not back at the head offices, that you have access to the information you need to use your intuition to make the right decisions." The result, Carlzon argues, is that business has to rethink completely how it is organized, so that many people can share decision-making power once consolidated at the top of the pyramid.

"The only real resource you have is the customer who is prepared to pay for what you offer," Carlzon believes. "If you understand that, then you place the customer at the top of every organizational chart you have. And next to the customers you put the people who are out there working with them, who face the customer every day. And you give these people the freedom and responsibility, and the authority, to make decisions on the spot on behalf of the company.

"Then you see that the administration—the head office—who used to be the people at the top of the organizational chart, should be repositioned at the bottom. We should be the support troops for the people at the front lines out there with the customers."

In the new vision Carlzon offers, management has a radically different purpose: to service those who meet face to face with the customer, doing whatever is needed to allow those people to represent the company.

✳✦✳
ADAPTATION FOR SURVIVAL

CREATIVITY, of course, means more than just the big breakthrough. Companies also need to develop steady practices of making small improvements and refinements to products and services. Paradoxically, the source of some of the best ideas in the world is found in hallowed tradition. There is no better example of this than Japan.

In Japan some of the most creative people spend their time meticulously adapting and refining existing ideas. This process of continuous fixes and adjustments produces beautiful and extraordinarily successful products. It's a different way of creating, with distinct cultural origins.

Kenneth Kraft, a professor of Buddhist studies at Lehigh University, sits in the Daisen-in Temple in Kyoto, in a garden so revered in Japan that it is listed as a national treasure.

"Japan is a very small country with limited space, so for practical reasons they had to figure out quite early how to do certain things in limited space," Kraft observes. "This garden, for example, is only twelve feet wide and forty-seven feet long. In photographs it looks bigger, but it's very small. And yet within this enclosed space, they've created an entire landscape."

The notion underlying the garden is of seeing a limited space as a very large area—even as a symbol of the universe itself. That idea has its background in Zen philosophy.

"One can see here, in this garden, that at a very early point in Japanese culture, the whole notion of miniaturization was quite highly developed," Kraft notes. "If you look carefully, you see that a sense of depth is created by the rocks in the background. Although just set back by a thin bit of gravel, they somehow seem quite far away, though in fact they're almost within reach. The Japanese have seen that through miniaturization they can accomplish quite a lot in a very small space."

Zen garden at Daisen-in Temple in Kyoto.

There are many other aspects of Japanese culture in which miniaturization is the organizing principle—from bonsai trees to hand-held video cameras and recorders. Just as a Zen garden seems to contain a whole universe, these minute electronic products compress into an extraordinarily small space a world of technological power.

"Another aspect of this garden that is revealing is the kind of adaptation that it shows. The Japanese are quite skilled at adapting. During the era this garden was built, Japan was highly influenced by China. But whenever Japan borrowed something from China, it didn't just simply take it in and discard whatever was there originally. It usually was able to develop the borrowed element alongside the indigenous element, and then combine them in very new ways.

Cutting a stencil for a textile design.

"We have the image of Japan as a kind of international shopper, just picking the best of any culture it is exposed to. But it's actually quite a bit more complex than that. To take something from one culture to another means you have to adapt it to the new circumstances. You can't borrow without adapting—and the adaptation can be very creative."

For example, the making of stencils for textile designs is a tradition over a thousand years old in Japan. It has been used for centuries to make patterns for kimonos. The same stencil-design techniques were also applied to the manufacture of handmade paper; Japanese wallpaper is still made this way.

As the market for handmade paper declined, one company, Kyotek in Kyoto, switched to the manufacture of exquisitely detailed printed circuits for computers. The expertise was the same; the product was entirely new. In the same way, Japanese ceramics companies have led the way in developing new, high-tech uses for ceramics, drawing on and adapting the ancient methods of Japanese potters.

Thus Kyotek and many other Japanese companies are not only preserving traditional skills, but going on to create new products that come out of those traditions—a necessary adaptation for survival in a competitive world marketplace.

The Creative Spirit

⊙
WORKER BEES
AND EXPLORER BEES

A CREATIVE COMPANY strikes a balance between those with an innovative bent and those who keep everything running. A blend of the two is optimal. "There's a natural tension between what you might call 'law-and-order' corporate types and creative people," says Jan Carlzon of SAS. "The law-and-order people are controllers who want a business to run according to fixed rules and routines, to be predictable and so on. For them 'freedom' is freedom from experiments, from uncertainty. Their outlook is naturally at odds with the adventure-seeking creative types.

"A vibrant company needs both. But they have to do more than respect each other: they need to understand each other. I've been working a lot with this in my own company. For a time we had a wildly creative situation—it was like Christmas every day for the creative people.

"Then the pendulum started to swing as the law-and-order people got things under control. And things ended up where everything was too controlled—you couldn't breathe. So I tried to create a balance rather than having the pendulum swing too far again.

"In a beehive there are different kinds of bees: workers and explorers. There are several other kinds, but for me those are the two most important. The explorer bees are the creative bees of the hive. They continually fly around to find new sources of pollen. When they find one, they fly back to the hive and give a signal to the other bees to tell them where the new discovery is.

"Then the worker bees fly out in a very well-ordered, controlled fashion and bring back the pollen. But the explorer bees don't comprehend the signals that tell the worker bees to harvest the pollen; they are designed just to fly around and explore.

"That's the balance I'd like to create in a company: where we respect each other and understand that we need both the creative entrepreneurs and the law-and-order people to have a productive company."

Each time you interact with the person on your "trouble list," make note of the VOJ criticisms that come to mind. Taking note of these criticisms allows you to get some distance from them, and this new perspective eventually enables you to give them up.

At the same time, bear in mind that progressive insights into how you and this other person can move forward may be embedded in these criticisms. Here's where you can draw upon your compassion. This evokes a spirit that allows you to rephrase and reformulate the criticism so that it becomes an insight rather than an insult. ✐

GO TO PAGE 142
↝

A Safe Haven for Ideas

☞*
VANQUISHING NEGATIVITY

APART FROM the structure of a company, the attitudes that pervade its operations can enhance or thwart creativity. One of the keys is building feelings of trust and respect to the point that people feel secure enough to express new ideas without fear of censure. This is because in the marketplace, imaginative thoughts have financial value. Everything from credit cards and microchips to ice cream cones and jumbo jets was once just someone's bright idea. An unimaginative, unreceptive attitude destroys opportunity.

Consider a classic example. It was in 1878 that Western Union turned down rights to the telephone. The reason the firm gave: "What use could the company make of an electric toy?" Not only the telephone, but also the radio and the personal computer were originally thought to have no commercial potential.

The voice of critical judgment kills such inspirations. The epitome of this negative way of thinking is the statement by Charles H. Duell, commissioner of the U.S. Office of Patents, who in 1899 said in a report to President McKinley, "Everything that can be invented has been invented." Duell argued that the Patent Office should be abolished.

It is the company or business person who is open to possibility and to dreams who can seize the ripe opportunity. Only through that openness can one gain the competitive advantage offered by innovation.

There are two key forces in the workplace that either oppose or encourage such creativity. One is the attitude toward innovation that people carry within themselves, and the other is the organizational climate. If the two are aligned, then change is effortless; if they are not—and they often are not—then the creative urge is stymied.

"Who the hell wants to hear actors talk?"
—HARRY M. WARNER, president of Warner Brothers pictures, in 1927

The workplace equivalent of the inner voice of judgment is the boss or co-worker who squelches a promising idea. Part of the power of naysayers to destroy a creative insight comes from the fragility of inspiration. So often the person who has a truly creative new idea also harbors doubts about its worth—a natural ambivalence. But if that person then brings up the idea in a close-minded environment, the creative spark dies then and there.

"Say you have the temerity to go into work with some great new idea," says Stanford's Michael Ray. "But when you tell it to some co-worker you respect, he tells you, 'Be careful, you're on thin ice. The Christmas bonuses are coming up; you might lose your job with a crazy idea like that.' I've seen over and over again in business that when you have an original idea, the first reaction to it is derision. That's a signal: you really know you're on to something when people are attacking your idea. If you push it a little further, people will say that it is obvious. And if you develop it even further, so that it is clear it works, then they'll say it was *their* idea."

That's why Ray suggests that people who work together agree to control the knee-jerk negativity that so often greets a new idea. Another way to counter the voice of criticism is by encouraging "naive" questions that call attention to unexamined assumptions in the workplace. Such questions, though they may seem naive, are never "dumb"—they challenge people to examine the habitual mind-set that makes work routine and uninspired.

"When you ask questions in the business world that are really getting to the heart of the matter," says Ray, "the typical reaction is a blank stare, or a non-answer like 'Because that's the way we've always done things around here.' What that tells you is that you've asked a very good 'dumb' question, because people often don't really know why they've been doing things that way."

Once the voice of criticism is stilled, what emerges is a spirit of hopefulness and optimism that sees a setback simply as information that will make the next attempt more likely to succeed.

"The horse is here to stay, but the automobile is only a novelty—a fad."
—PRESIDENT OF THE MICHIGAN SAVINGS BANK advising Henry Ford's lawyer not to invest in the Ford Motor Company

"Heavier than air flying machines are impossible."
—LORD KELVIN, 1895

"Video won't be able to hold on to any market it captures after the first six months. People will soon get tired of staring at a plywood box every night."
—DARYL F. ZANUCK, head of 20th Century Fox movie studio, commenting on television in 1946

YES AND NO

I always compare any idea to a golden wire," says animator Chuck Jones. "It's really gorgeous, a lovely thing, but also a bit fragile.

"You come trotting in with this idea, and it's a YES . . . and 'yes' means contribute, help me—I need help to get the strength to survive.

"And then when we come up with what a NO looks like, it's a monolithic, ugly thing. It's made of cement.

"But some people have made their entire reputations—become presidents of motion picture companies—by saying no! It's one of the most horrible words in the English language. This no can destroy an idea, because you have this fragile little yes trying to survive...

"Anybody can drop that monstrous NO on the yes before it even has a chance for life."

✺ⓖ✺
DARING TO BE POSITIVE

I F PEOPLE are to persevere despite obstacles, they have to stop imagining all the reasons why something can't work and start thinking about all the ways that they can *make* it work. Stanford's Jim Collins says, "My MBA students are tremendously good at shooting down business ideas. I'll present a case study of an entrepreneur and they'll say, 'This is wrong, this is no good, that is why it won't work.' They'll give me dozens of reasons why an entrepreneur will fail."

Then the entrepreneur visits the class. "And he'll say, 'Yes, all those reasons you give are true. But we moved ahead anyway and figured out fifteen ways to overcome those fifteen problems and make it all work.' "

The best response to a negative mind-set that shoots down new ideas is one that says a daring vision *can* work with some creative solutions. Would-be innovators must be bold enough to dismiss the voices of fear and doubt. "You can't be constantly worried about what happens if I try this and it doesn't work," says Collins. "You may not know all the ways you'll make the business work, or how you'll get your product on the market. But if you're committed to it, the probabilities change in your favor."

When Nolan Bushnell was president of Atari, the pioneering video game company, he got the idea for the game Breakout while on vacation. At Atari, people were encouraged to be frank with one another, and when he described to his colleagues his idea for a video game, the response was brutally frank—and overwhelmingly negative.

But he had a clear vision of what the game could be like, and went ahead anyway. "The common wisdom in the game companies at that time was that games with paddles were passé," said Bushnell. "But I knew in my mind that the game was going to be fun."

So Bushnell went out on a limb and hired a consultant to develop a prototype of the game. Once people at Atari could play the game, their skepticism changed to enthusiasm. Breakout went on to be one of the best-selling video games of all time.

Sometimes an intuitive idea can be so powerful that it leads a person to radically change his life. Take the case of Lou Krouse. He was in his twenty-fifth year with the phone company as a middle manager when he got a bright idea—one so compelling that he quit to start his own business.

The problem he tackled was this: about twenty percent of American households have no bank account. The people in these, the poorest of households, can't write checks. To pay a phone bill, for instance, they have to take the time to go to the company office and pay in cash, or buy a money order at a dollar and a half.

Krouse's vision was of a system of electronic machines in stores where people without bank accounts could pay their utility bills conveniently, near their homes and without extra costs. For the stores it would mean hundreds of extra customers coming through the door. For the utilities it would mean receiving their payments with minimum fuss.

But to make his dream a reality, Krouse had to travel the country looking for backing. He was within a month of personal bankruptcy when he finally found a bank that would invest, letting him hook up to their automatic money machines in return for a stake in his business.

Within three years, Krouse's company, National Payments Network, had revenues of 26 million dollars a year, with three and a half million customers in nineteen states.

VALUING INTUITION

THE CAPACITY for making intuitive decisions is a basic ingredient of creativity. Intuition means relinquishing control of the thinking mind and trusting the vision of the unconscious. Because it can't be quantified or rationally justified, it is often opposed in the workplace. But it has the ring of truth, because it is grounded in the ability of the unconscious to organize information into unanticipated new ideas.

"Intuition is what you add to the information you collect," says SAS's Jan Carlzon. "If you understand that, you see you can never collect total information. You have to add your feelings, your gut reaction, to make the

OILING THE CREATIVE SPIRIT

One way to encourage people to take creative risks is by rewarding them for it. That is the approach taken by Tom Melohn, former head of North American Tool and Die.

Every month Melohn gave cash bonuses for innovations and extra efforts. One bonus winner was Jim Norsworthy, a shop maintenance worker. Norsworthy's innovation dealt with problems created by the large and expensive quantities of oil used by the company—oil that could become toxic waste. Norsworthy heard about an oil-recycling device with an ingenious filter system that allowed oil to be reused instead of thrown out. He stuck his neck out to get one; the machine paid for itself within a week.

By rewarding such individual efforts to innovate, Melohn turned what had been a sleepy metal-stamping plant into a model company with sales up more than twenty-five percent each year, and a return on investment equivalent to the top ten percent of the Fortune 500 firms.

right decision. In that sense, there is no answer that's right for everybody—just what's right for you. That's using intuition in the right way."

One of the forces that makes a strong intuitive sense even more valuable is that the world is heading toward a single global arena—or so argues Carlzon. "Although it is most obvious in Europe, everywhere in the world you see the same trend toward the elimination of borders," he says. "You see it in business and economics, in culture, in food, what have you. The only borders that will remain are political." Operating a business in that global arena demands innovative ways of understanding and responding to the needs of different cultures and peoples. Very often a single decision will not accommodate the different needs of, say, the Swedes, the Italians, and the Japanese.

"That's where you have to calculate in your intuitions about people—your sense of their reactions, their feelings," says Carlzon. Business people who know how to listen to their customers rather than just study figures and statistics will have a splendid future in a competitive global economy, Carlzon believes.

"Unfortunately, schools don't teach us to trust our intuition. Instead they teach a sort of absolute knowledge. We teach students to look for one right answer, which they will discover through gathering complete information. But in real life you find that even after you gather all the relevant information, there is still a gap, a part that you cannot neatly calculate. And that's where you have to add your intuition to make your final decision and go ahead.

"We also make a mistake in schools by measuring performance in absolute terms. We teach in terms of specific answers, in inches, in pounds, in specific right or wrong quantities. And we grade accordingly. But we never tell students about what lies beyond the range of absolutes, about the uncertainties you constantly deal with in real life.

"So I think we should teach both approaches to knowing—the absolute kind of measurement and the knowledge that intuition brings."

Says Anita Roddick, "No market research in the world is going to tell you why people don't want to buy this product or why they love your company. But if you have your intuition working, you can look at a huge marketing research report from the cosmetics industry and just know, 'This is wrong.' "

Roddick tells of getting a report on marketing trends that said the growth of sales for baby products was going to be minor. "But our intuition told us that was plain wrong," she recalls. "So many women on our staff and so many women we knew were having babies, that we just had a hunch that the baby market would be much bigger than the projections predicted. So we dug down, went back with our own questions, and looked again. We found that the real figures were about four times greater than the research had shown. That's intuition at work."

RISK IS IN THE EYE OF THE BEHOLDER

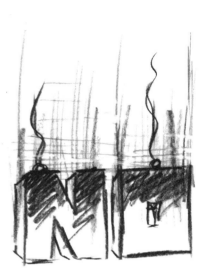

R ISK, LIKE BEAUTY, is in the eye of the beholder. A business venture that may seem risky or dangerous from the outside can seem entirely different to the person in its midst. The hidden variable is commitment.

As the Body Shop's Anita Roddick says, "I don't think I'm a risk-taker. I don't think any entrepreneur is. I think that's one of those myths of commerce. The new entrepreneur is more values-led: you do what looks risky to other people because that's what your convictions tell you to do. Other companies would say I'm taking risks, but that's my path—it doesn't feel like risk to me."

Committing to starting a business is a classic odds changer. The case of the Giro helmet is instructive. Jim Gentis was a bicycle racer who invented an entirely new design for the bike helmet. His passion was bicycle racing, but he hated the bulky, heavy helmets that racers had to wear. At fourteen ounces, the hard-shell models weighed too much, had all the aerodynamics of a clunky army helmet, and made a racer too sweaty.

Gentis had no money set aside to start a business, but he knew that he wanted a new kind of helmet and was determined to build it himself. So with a great deal of experimentation, Gentis found a new design for a much sleeker, more aerodynamic helmet that had all the structural strength of the old army-helmet designs. He used the same basic material, polystyrene.

But when it came to capping the polystyrene with a good-looking, sturdy protective shell, he was stumped. The material he wanted to use was an ultra-light plastic. But the cost of the machine to manufacture it would be $80,000—which he did not have. After much experimentation, and by now somewhat desperate, Gentis finally came up with a Lycra covering that could be produced in a wide array of colors and designs.

Gentis had no capital for starting a company. By all standards, he hadn't a chance. But starting with just a few sales to friends, the helmet caught on. The Giro helmet offered bike afficionados the safety they needed, yet let them be stylish and pick a helmet that matched their outfit. An instant hit, the Giro has dominated the bike helmet market since it was introduced. Gentis's commitment changed the probabilities.

A LEAP OF FAITH

FOR LARRY WILSON of the Pecos River Learning Center, the trouble is this: "If you always do what you've always done, you'll always get what you've always got." That produces zero growth, stagnation.

The antidote is the realization that: "You'll always do what you've always done if you always think the way you've always thought." For that reason, says Wilson, "we help people think about risks differently, so they're not as fearful. You can't always get rid of all the anxiety surrounding risk, but you can reduce it a lot."

Perhaps the best data on reducing the anxiety of risk-taking comes from research on parachute jumpers. University of Massachusetts psychologist Seymour Epstein measured the anxiety levels in novice and expert parachutists as they prepared for a jump.

The expert jumpers were calm as they packed their chutes, got in the plane, and as it took off and climbed thousands of feet to the altitude from which they would leap into thin air. They reported little anxiety until the minutes just before the jump, as they were preparing to leap from the plane.

The novices, however, experienced mounting anxiety at every step of the way: as they packed their chutes, boarded the plane, rode higher and higher. For them, the mere anticipation of what they were about to do led to a crescendo of jangled nerves. Though they had yet to make the jump, in their minds they had already leapt time and again—to disaster.

No matter what the arena may be, the anxiety that builds in anticipation of risk-taking springs from exaggerated fantasies of failure and catastrophe. Fear of risk-taking in the workplace works much the same way: *If I bring up this new idea,* you tell yourself, *and it flops, then I'll make a fool of myself at the meeting.* Your boss will see you as incompetent, and pass you by for the promotion or raise you want. Even worse, your mind tells you: *In the coming wave of cuts and consolidations, my job will be the first to go.* And because you'll be fired, you'll never be able to get another position. And you won't be able to make the payments on your car, or your house, or anything. Before you know it, you envision yourself living like a bag lady on a sidewalk grate.

So you shut up and say nothing. Better safe than sorry, you tell yourself, and curl up and hide in that comfort zone.

That is the power of the Ropes Course zip line. As you stand there waiting your turn, the mind can easily turn on its catastrophe generator. You can picture yourself paralyzed for life, living out your days in a hospital bed . . . then you somehow find the courage to let go anyway, to make the leap.

You need a certain degree of faith to take such plunges. And that plunge is an eloquent metaphor for the leaps that are demanded by the creative organization.

More Than Just a Job

℘

CLOUDS ON THE FLOOR

DIFFERENT APPROACH to stimulating creative life in the workplace is through people's physical surroundings. A barren, institutionalized office suggests a barren, institutional way of looking at things. By the same token, rich and varied surroundings are conducive to creative thinking.

At SAS headquarters, for instance, there are activities designed to lift people's spirits—for example, string quartets playing at lunch hour. Explains company president Carlzon, "We want people to feel appreciated and respected, because we know that people who feel that way will do a better job for the company."

For Anita Roddick, the very aesthetics of an office can be a stimulant to the imagination. "I used to be a teacher, and I know that one way to encourage creativity is to make the environment stimulating, even entertaining. So walking around our office is a visual and sensory experience unlike most any other office at a normal company.

"Everywhere you turn, on the walls are posters and charts and photos that celebrate the human spirit—not charts about profit lines and productivity and how much money we're making. We borrow great thoughts, great images, that show what we mean—everything from the words of Chief Seattle to that wonderful photo exhibition, The Family of Man. We put them up all around, so that's what you see as your interruption from work. The aesthetics of a company are a way to open up the spirit.

"In our offices, everyone has to go down a very long, very narrow corridor into one of the big warehouses. We've tried to make that stimulating, with wonderful photos of indigenous peoples around the world who are our trading partners. And I have watched people walk down that corridor and I noticed that people touch the wall as they go.

"So we're toying with adding textures and sounds to the visuals: getting slit bamboo, pipes, rubber suction cups, anything that makes a sound. So as you walk down this corridor, you can actually make sounds—press something and it whizzes or pops. It's a totally silly idea, which would be wonderful for six-year-olds. But I want to experiment with it to see how you can make going to work just a little bit more exciting.

"The same applies to our shops. I don't want to go into my shops and be bored. If I'm bored, God help me—my customers are going to be bored, too. So you continually try to work out what would surprise them—a different display, or the sound of running water, or the staff in completely different uniforms.

"We're trying to get people to fall in love with change. So everything's always changing in the atmosphere of the company. Tomorrow all the notice boards are going to be different from today."

The idea of keeping the senses alive and guessing is actually built into the architecture of Enator, a consulting firm in Sweden whose product is ideas and solutions to its clients' problems. If creativity involves turning things upside-down and inside-out, Enator is architectually designed to help workers stay mentally fresh. "I think it's stimulating to come to work in an office building where you are continually on a voyage of discovery," says Hans Larson, Enator's president.

To cultivate the bent of mind that is ready to grapple with problems, the very design of the company's building is bedeviling. People confront perceptual and physical "problems" at every turn—literally. In the Enator building there are no rectangular rooms; the layout is one of odd angles and shapes. There is no space that the mind meets with lazy recognition; wherever the eyes fall, they meet the unexpected:

⬤ On the floor, a surrealistic depiction of a cloud-filled sky

⬤ On the walls, trompe l'oeil paintings that suggest three-dimensional bars where there is only flat surface

⬤ Portholes and panes of glass in places that offer surprising vistas of activity in other rooms or floors

⬤ Corridors that zigzag, without straight lines, and that take you past a melange of geometric shapes—circles, cubes, trapezoids

⬤ Rooms that break convention, such as a meeting room where people

have their conversations and meals at a table made from a grand piano.

What's more, there are none of the usual visual guides—no nameplates on doors, no signs announcing where you are. If you want to find someplace or someone, you have to ask. That forces people to ask questions, to talk to one another. People are constantly meeting, talking, engaging with one another. And from those meetings spring unpredictable connections.

Another advantage is that the building itself fosters the kind of spontaneous interactions that are critical to teamwork. Says one of the employees at Enator, "It's very easy to get locked up in one way of looking at something, so we spend lots of time bouncing ideas off each other. If this were a traditional building, it just wouldn't happen as easily, because it's much harder to get up and walk down a corridor to another cubicle and sit down. Here it's easy: all the spaces throw you together."

That fellowship is strengthened by the company atmosphere. Hans Larson says, "We believe in building a second home for our people." And just like at home, people feel free to be themselves. As another Enator consultant put it, "The building reflects an attitude that it's okay to seem to be doing nothing. People trust that you're thinking things over. You don't have to be guilty about taking a coffee break here."

MORE LIKE A FAMILY

WHEN IT COMES TO melding a harmonious team, managers eventually learn that one of the ingredients is something rarely associated with the workplace: love.

"Love is not a word people talk about easily," says Larry Wilson. "Yet, increasingly we're seeing that people are wanting to know that somebody cares about them, that they are not just seen as some interchangeable part. Real leadership is about demonstrating that your intention is to care for people and to support their growth.

"Leadership is about three things. One is creating a vision that you can believe in and communicate to others. Second is guiding your people

THE SPIRIT OF CARING

The power of people to care about their fellow workers—and to find creative solutions to human problems—is exemplified by the case of Randy Theis, an employee of the Des Moines Water Works. Theis contracted cancer, and a series of operations forced him to use up all his sick leave, which put enormous financial pressure on him and his family of five children.

Costs for health insurance were skyrocketing at the company; there was no possibility of extending the number of sick days allowed Theis. Then a group of fellow employees had the idea of donating their own sick leave days to Theis. The company changed its regulations to allow it, and twenty-five fellow workers signed up.

As James Autry says of this incident in his book *Love and Profit*: "We managers have the opportunity to lead and direct people in that ever more powerful bond of common enterprise, and at the same time to create a place of friendship, deep personal connections, and neighborhood."

Autry adds: "How about this for a new management bumper sticker: IF YOU'RE NOT CREATING COMMUNITY, YOU'RE NOT MANAGING."

OPPOSITE: *The lobby of the Enator building in Sweden: a visually provocative and paradoxical design.*

IAN OLSSON

KINDNESS IS NOT ENOUGH

Doug Greene, founder and CEO of New Hope Communications, started by telling the people at his company that the three rules of his business were: "Be kind, be kind, be kind." But then he noticed that people started being a bit dishonest in order to be kind. So he changed it to: "Be kind, be honest, be kind," and finally to: "Be kind, be honest, have fun."

toward that vision. And the third is the growth and development of those you lead, without regard for the consequences of that growth for yourself.

"That third goal is a form of love, of caring. Whatever word you use, knowing they have that kind of support makes people more willing to be risk-takers. We all have had that kind of experience, whether it was with a parent or teacher or mentor at work. A leader's job is to stretch us and take us further than we think we can go.

"Increasingly, as we realize that *people* are our most important competitive advantage, we see that we have to help people grow. You don't do that on a large scale; you do it in small teams. You can have one or two thousand teams, but each should have six to ten people. That team becomes the center of caring. And, if you can get a team of people to come together and care for one another, you have returned to the scale of the family. They are less vulnerable to fear and anxiety and freer to let their creativity emerge."

The new information environment, as Jan Carlzon of SAS envisions it, demands a new style of management. "The business leader of the future is more like a mother or father in a family or a coach for a team. You have to create an atmosphere in which people feel that they are respected, that you have faith in them, even that you love them. You have to manage by love.

"And by doing so you will help people achieve their full potential, dare to take risks, and dare to use their intuition to make decisions. And they can do it because they know that even if they fail sometimes, they will be accepted and will get a new chance.

"Whereas if you manage people by fear, you will see how people shrink and perform far below their capability. And that will not create any profitability or competitiveness for your company."

Being preoccupied with worries distracts people from focusing on their work. This kind of anxiety is a creativity killer. The antidote is a workplace where people can be relaxed. Having just such an easygoing atmosphere in his company comes naturally to Yvon Chouinard, the head of Patagonia.

"I told myself I was going to be a businessman who didn't have to go to work nine to five. If the surf was up I could take off and go surfing anytime."

"You want to have a climate in the company where people feel comfortable," he says. "Then they're willing to open themselves up and throw out crazy ideas and nobody laughs. Or everybody laughs, but you feel, so what—and shrug it off.

"You can't separate creativity from risk-taking. I think the best ideas are so whacko, and so ahead of their time, that everybody's going to laugh at them. So people have to feel confident enough to just throw it out anyway, and not be hurt if nobody likes it."

One of the ways the men and women of Patagonia are made to feel comfortable is by having a daycare center on the premises. "A mother can drop her kid off at quarter to eight, go to work, and then come have lunch with her kid," says Chouinard. "Or they can just go back and forth to the daycare center all day long. We even have some mothers who let their kids play next to their desk for a while."

Isn't that a disruption? Quite the contrary, says Chouinard: "It frees up the parents so they don't have to worry about their kids all day long. Then they can just concentrate on working. Getting rid of the hassles in people's lives leaves them free to be creative. Whatever we pay to subsidize the daycare center pays for itself a thousand times over through more productivity."

The aim is simple: "The more the workplace feels like being at home, the more people feel they're in a group they enjoy being with, the more people can focus on the particular direction the company wants to go in," Chouinaird believes. "It becomes a movement rather than a business, and that makes it extremely productive."

A *Patagonia employee visits the on-site daycare center to nurse her baby.*

✻◎✻
A DIFFERENT BOTTOM LINE

IMAGINE AN ENVIRONMENT where the process of work matters as much as its product. In such a company you don't focus just on results: how you get there is as important as where you go. That switch in perspec-

Wrestling with the VOJ

THERE ARE times when we are tied into knots by anxiety and self-doubt. At that moment our minds are so jammed with negative chatter that we cannot proceed with what we want to do. When things get really bad, try the following concentration technique. It takes only a minute or two.

☙ Sit comfortably with your back straight, close your eyes, and breathe quietly. Now begin to sense the skin all over your body. Notice how it covers every part of your body, every contour, every muscle.

Now imagine that there is nothing inside of your skin. Instead, your skin is just a thin membrane covering empty space. Take a few moments to experience the sense of openness and emptiness inside you. Keep experiencing that for one or two minutes more.

Upon repeated use, this "empty body" technique becomes a practical way of getting out of the clutches of the VOJ. ☙

If this exercise is a bit too passive for your taste, or if you just can't sit still, try vigorous exercise. Research indicates that aerobic exercise, which accelerates the heart rate and breathing and increases oxygen levels in the tive transforms the very meaning of work; with such an orientation people grow as part of their work.

There is a growing gap between what many businesses see as their purpose and what more and more people want in their work. The larger that gap, the more alienated people feel from their work. And the more alienated they feel, the less of their creative energy is available.

The unfortunate result is that too many businesses are relying on a combination of economic incentives (the carrot) and fear (the stick) to spur their workers. But that particular combination of motives has a deadening effect on creativity. Personal creativity flows when work is done largely for the sheer pleasure of it, not because of external pressure.

Many workers are no longer in search of a job that is simply a source of wealth, status, and power, but rather one that—apart from assuring a decent living—offers a sense of meaning and a platform for individual creativity. Production as an end in itself satisfies neither of those desires. If a business fails to recognize this, it may find it difficult to get or keep the best people.

One way to heal that breach, as well as benefit both companies and the people who work for them, is to invest in developing the inner resources of workers. This solution has been embraced by some forward-looking business leaders who redefine the purpose of their companies beyond just making a profit to making the workplace an arena for the personal growth of those who work there. That's not to say, of course, that a company should not be profitable—just that it should widen its focus from an exclusive fixation on the bottom line, at the expense of the quality of work itself.

Anita Roddick puts it this way: "I don't want our success to be measured only by financial yardsticks, or by our distribution or number of shops. What I want to be celebrated for—and it's going to be tough in a business environment—is how good we are to our employees and how we benefit our community. It's a different bottom line."

One of the most promising models for business, Roddick suggests, is an old one. "Look what the Quakers did: they didn't create a huge distance between management and workers. They looked after their employees—

they provided houses, even built towns. They were honorable people; they didn't take more out of the business than they put in. They made profits, of course. But they didn't tell lies, and they valued labor. That's an attitude we should get back to. We've come to see education for the work force as an expense rather than an investment.

"And beyond the needs of the work force, business has to consider its dealings with the community. It's not enough just to be a rich neighbor providing jobs. You should look after other neighbors to be a truly successful business in the community. That means that you do more than provide a place where there are Monday-to-Friday jobs. You make it a workplace that enhances people's lives—their communications, their marriages, their family life."

Roddick believes that this approach is going to become part of the mainstream. The reason: "People in the workplace are saying, 'I want to work for a company that values me, not just the bottom line on the balance sheet. I want to work for a company that enhances the human spirit, creates friendships, gives me a sense of being alive.' Because that's what we all want: to be alive in the workplace."

blood, is helpful in fighting the depression associated with feelings of low self-esteem. Many people find that running, cycling, and swimming not only relieve depression but also help cleanse their minds of nagging judgments.

Another way of dealing with the VOJ is by putting it into perspective. You can do this by poking fun at it. The following exercise may help.

☜ Shut your eyes and imagine that you can hear and see a negative statement you regularly make about yourself, e.g. , "I never have an original idea."

When you have this thought in mind, begin to intensify and enlarge it. Make it more and more strident. Have it flash on and off in brilliant neon lights.

Continue to make the statement bigger, louder, and more elaborate— using laser lights, screaming rockets, full symphony orchestras, and choruses of disapproval. Let the ridiculousness of this scene sink in.

Open your eyes. ☜

When some people do this exercise, they become instantly aware of how puny their VOJ is without their support. We alone supply the energy, light, and power on which the VOJ thrives.

A passing note on the judgments of others: One of Babe Ruth's rivals said that he was making a big mistake by dropping pitching to move to a position where he could bat in the lineup every day. And in 1945, Vannevar Bush, an adviser to the president of the United States, warned, "The atomic bomb will never go off, and I speak as an expert in explosives."

GO TO PAGE 154

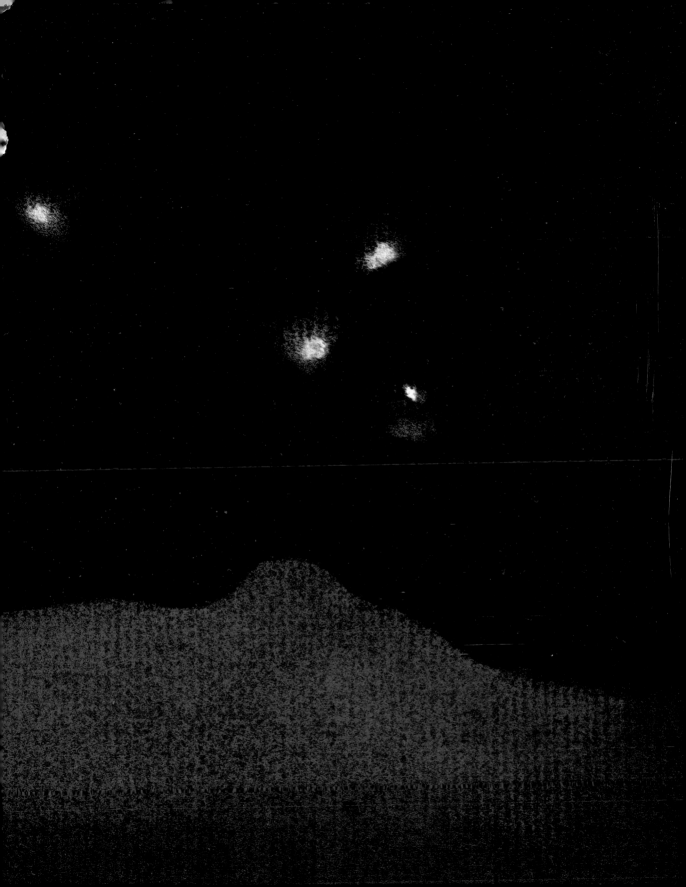

CHAPTER FOUR

Creating Community

"It was the best of times, it was the worst of times. It was the age of wisdom, it was the age of foolishness. It was the epoch of belief, it was the epoch of incredulity. It was the season of light. It was the season of darkness. It was the Spring of hope. It was the Winter of despair. We had everything before us. We had nothing before us. We were all going direct to Heaven. We were all going direct the other way."

—Charles Dickens

A Tale of Two Cities

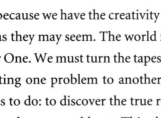

Mother Teresa with Dean James Parks Morton of the Cathedral of St. John the Divine.

MARY BLOOM

DICKENS wrote about the age of the French Revolution, but his words speak to us now. We also teeter between hope and despair, between light and darkness. The global upsurge of ethnic and religious diversity now forces us to think more creatively about a future political order. The ecological crisis demands that each of us examine how our comfortable daily habits affect the health and survival of all other beings on the planet. Malnutrition, disease, addiction, and homelessness are so widespread that none of us is immune from their effects or exempt from reflecting upon their causes.

Yet it is also the spring of hope because we have the creativity to solve all of these problems, as intractable as they may seem. The world is much like the tapestry described in Chapter One. We must turn the tapestry over in order to find the threads connecting one problem to another. That's what these revolutionary times ask us to do: to discover the true relationships between things so that we can solve our problems. This chapter is about people who are relieving the suffering of their fellow human beings. To do this, they are transforming old institutions and creating new ones to deal imaginatively with complex, interconnected problems.

Martin Luther King said: "Every man must decide whether he will walk in the light of creative altruism or in the darkness of destructive selfishness. This is the judgment. Life's most persistent and urgent question is, What are you doing for others?"

Altruism springs from our instinct to help others, the opposite disposition from "I'm just doing my job and to hell with everyone else." Although altruistic sentiments are noble, they can remain just pieties in the sky unless they are translated into practical action. Altruism needs to be linked with our creative ability to solve problems.

The Institute for Noetic Sciences in Sausalito, California, presents annual awards to people who embody unselfish service and whose work offers an innovative solution to a pressing human problem. The recipients of these awards include:

● **Celeste Tate,** who founded Gleaners, a food bank that collects unsold food from grocery stores and distributes it in special supermarkets where people can pay just $2 or work in exchange for a bag of food. Gleaners now feeds twenty thousand people each month.

● **Janet Marchese,** adoptive mother of a baby with Down's syndrome, who began putting the parents of Down's children together with couples who wanted to adopt them. Her Down's Syndrome Adoption Network has placed over 1,500 children, and has a waiting list of couples who want to adopt.

● **Falaka and David Fatah,** a couple who headed off their son's descent into the underworld of a street gang by inviting the gang to live in their own home. Today the House of Umoja, in Philadelphia, fills twenty-four renovated row houses, and has given a home and guidance to over two thousand young men who have been convicted in juvenile courts.

Winston Franklin, Executive Vice-President of the Institute for Noetic Sciences, explains that "these are ordinary people who saw problems in their neighborhood or city and decided to do something about it. In each case, their only genius was their goodness, which seems to arise from a similarly deep place in each of them."

If I am not for myself, who will be for me? If I am not for others, what am I? And if not now, when?
—RABBI HILLEL, 12TH CENTURY

"There are three things: Faith, Hope, and Love. But the greatest of these is Love."
—CORINTHIANS 13:13

A Natural Interdependence

SYSTEMS SCIENTIST George Land also believes that the ability to generate radically innovative solutions to problems comes from a deep place: nature. Land believes that all of human civilization is moving into a distinctly new phase of social organization. After years spent carefully observing the kinship between natural change and cultural invention, his view is that the clue to our future is already visible in nature.

Systems scientist George Land.

Land's theory is that whether creativity happens over millions of years, in plants and animals, or whether it happens in a few minutes when a human being solves a problem, it follows the same master pattern. The parallelism of nature and culture is found in three distinct phases of organization through which all living systems pass. In the first phase, after exploring all sorts of options, the system essentially invents itself. In the second, the system establishes a formal pattern based on what now works best. In the third phase, the living system has to break the boundaries of this established pattern in order to bring in what is new and continue to grow.

These phases can be seen in human development. The first phase approximates the early years of life, up to about age five. A child explores from moment to moment, almost without inhibition. Trying to learn to walk, he'll fall down fifty times, pick himself up, and dust himself off. He'll try any combination of words to learn a new language. And by the time he's about five, he has a sense of who he is.

When children go to school, society very carefully programs them to move into the second phase. Now they're less concerned about being inventive; rather, the effort goes to building a stable pattern, one consonant with the mores and folkways of society.

If successful, the pattern established in the second phase can last until late adulthood. But by then we've exhausted the pattern. We reach a point where nothing feels right. Perhaps we call it a "mid-life crisis." Regardless of what we label it, we know in the deepest part of our being that to survive we need to experiment, to strike out in a new direction. Land observes: "The invitation then is for us to get out of that basic pattern and to reach down inside and rediscover that five-year-old child. We have the opportunity to consciously sculpt our lives in ways that will allow us to open up to the full range of creativity that's available to all of us."

THE BALLAD OF OAK CREEK CANYON

GEORGE LAND has found a place where he believes traces of the three phases of creative change are visible. He points to Oak Creek Canyon, near Sedona, Arizona, as a kind of living textbook whose pages reveal powerful urges to create that reside in all of nature and in every one of us.

"What happened here in Sedona about five million years ago," he explains, "was that the crust of the earth opened up, and this canyon dropped down seven hundred feet, exposing layer after layer of rock. And it opened up a way for the deep springs that are in these mountains to flow through the canyon. In those layers of canyon wall we can see the playing out of the creative process over gigantic epochs of time.

"First, what had been unyielding rock began to break down, finer and finer, until it became soil, and a few plants could start to grab hold and grow. And then, in characteristic first-phase fashion, all kinds of grasses and bushes and trees came into the canyon." Like the entrepreneurial phase of an organization or a new community, this is a period of openness to many alternatives. But as some of those alternatives prove more fruitful than others, the range narrows.

In the case of the canyon, mesquite, manzanita, and juniper trees— just a few of the many varieties that came to the canyon—took over and

Crown of thorns.

created their own pattern. They essentially colonized the canyon, repro-
ducing themselves and pushing everything else out of the way.

A rainbow over Oak Creek Canyon.

"After a long period of time," explains Land, "the trees got in each
other's way. They started—literally—to kill each other. They were so successful that they used up the nutrients in the soil, crowded each other out,
and then started to die out. But they had prepared the way. Their very
failure was their success. They had created a new kind of environment, a
new kind of soil, enriching it by their fulfillment and their death. As they
died, their leaves provided new compost."

In the canyon's third phase, the old pattern awakened to new life. All
kinds of new species came in and created an interdependent ecology in the
canyon, one in which they made room for each other and allowed for new
varieties of life. For Land, the parallels to the evolution of human organization are clear. We are embarking on the third phase of community life;
we must now discover a way to integrate the diverse peoples and cultures
of the world into a new whole.

Precise Observation

PRECISE observation is another tool that can help you use your creativity. Precise observation is when you pay attention to things you hadn't noticed before or had taken for granted. This is essential when you are solving difficult and complex problems. You are precisely observing when you see with a delight that seems to brighten what you are seeing, giving every detail and aspect a startling clarity and presence. The ordinary becomes strange and exciting, just as it does when you are sightseeing in a brand new place. At the highest level, precise observation is akin to the "white moment," described on page 46. This is awareness of such clarity that the self-conscious I ordinarily present in perception evaporates. As with the Zen calligrapher, there's just "the doing."

Heuristic: Be Awake

SO OFTEN we go through our days on automatic pilot. To a certain degree, we like people and situations to be predictable; we enjoy the

RESCUING A RAIN FOREST

AS IF IN SUPPORT of Land's theory, new forms of collaboration, based upon a perceived interdependence, are being invented spontaneously by people all over the world. The visionary efforts of a group of Swedish schoolchildren are an example.

It began a few years back with the children in Ena Kern's class in a tiny school in the Swedish countryside. The children had learned that with the destruction of the rain forests in the Southern Hemisphere, many small animals were dying. Since many of the children had pets such as a dog or a rabbit, it was easy for them to grasp the problem. "The children were also very frustrated," recalls Kern, because "they felt they'd never have a chance to see the rain forests themselves, since by the time they were adults, the

NEWS OF THE
CREATIVE PAST

This story just in from Fifth Century Greece. A note from the science desk with a little human interest touch. There has been some concern about the great thinker, Democritus, the first person to conceive of the atomic structure of the universe. He has been observed sitting in the Public Square for days on end, apparently lost in thought. Concerned citizens called in Hippocrates, the town doctor. Well, the report is that he has examined Democritus and the worry is over. It turns out Democritus is actually stimulating his creativity by living inside his mind. Just a little meditation. Apparently when you are lost in thought some of your best ideas can be found.

forests would be gone."

Then a boy in her class made a simple but audacious suggestion: why don't we save the rain forest by buying it?

"All the children thought it was a very good idea—let's get enough money to buy a rain forest," says Kern. "But I didn't know what to do. How could you buy a rain forest? Then, just by accident, I met an American professor who had done research in an area called Monte Verde in Costa Rica. She told me they had a project there to raise money to buy and protect rain forests. So she came and visited with the children and showed them pictures of the rain forest that they could buy. And they were so excited they said, Let's start raising money and buy as much as we can. I could have said that's not possible, but I didn't."

So the children began to raise money. They organized country fairs, with events like pony riding, rabbit-jumping contests, and dog steeple chases. And they wrote songs about the rain forests and performed them in public:

Oh, you beautiful rain forest
Why do you have to die?
All species need you
We must prevent it!
You cannot be cut down!
We all need you.

Kern recalls of the children who conceived the project: "At first they said we can buy only a very little piece, but if we show others, they will help us and it can be a bigger piece and perhaps we can get very, very many people to help, and then it would be worth the work. And if children in all countries around the world raise money for rain forests, then we will succeed and there will be many rain forests left—not just that little piece. *That was the children's vision.*"

Soon schoolchildren across Sweden heard about the project, and thousands of them took up the effort—and the song. Even the King of Sweden came to the little school and backed the project.

"If you have a problem," says Kern, "ask the children for a solution and try it. That will change the world."

habitual and we like to avoid surprises. But there is a downside to routine. We can easily become fixed in our ways of seeing. Our expectation of how things are supposed to be replaces our seeing.

This can range from not seeing the new color or cut of your partner's hair to not seeing a new trend in consumer taste that could drastically affect your business.

Here are some ideas for refocusing your perceptions.

✎ Each day, do one thing different from your normal routine. You might go to bed at a new time, or take a new route to work or school. Or eat something you would never dream of eating. If you are feeling more adventurous, strike up a conversation with a particularly difficult person (maybe someone you really can't stand) and treat this person in a completely new way. The more pesky the person and entrenched the routine, the more likely you are to shake up your habitual ways of seeing things. The key is not to think about how to change things or to ask "What is the best way to change them?" but rather to change things for no other reason than just for the sake of it.

What we see every day becomes ordinary to us. People, things, sights, sounds, and smells seem to disappear from awareness. They lose their distinctiveness. One way of dealing with this is to invent a new pattern, a fresh way of seeing something quite commonplace.

✎ Begin with something as basic as water. The idea is to notice the number of times a day you come in contact with it and the extraordinary number of ways it appears in your life: from a hot shower or the delicate beads of mist on the leaves outside your window to the ice cubes clinking in your glass.

This technique of taking things out of their ordinary context and creating a new pattern for them is a way of making the familiar strange.

Another way of observing more precisely is to take in new kinds of information. Paying attention to a person's nonverbal behavior—their gestures, body language, posture, tone of voice—enlarges the field of perception. By doing this, we hear not just the words a person says but the "music" as well. This kind of observation is practiced by therapists, doctors, and investigators in a variety of situations where important information may be concealed intentionally or unintentionally. Dr. Alexa Canady, the neurosurgeon profiled in Chapter One, says that her creativity is in listening to what the patient is really saying—rather than simply accepting what they say at face value.

"Reflective listening" is an additional way to ensure that you are not shutting out useful information. Sometimes we drift away into our own thoughts while someone is talking to us. We often tune out as we mentally prepare our next response. ✊

✊ A way to counteract this all too natural tendency is to set yourself the task of mirroring the other person's conversation. Every so often let the other person know your impressions of what he is trying to communicate. The object is to reflect back to him all the details without interpreting or judg-

The Relief of Suffering

✊* AVANCE: REKINDLING HOPE

CREATIVITY comes from a person's inner being. If that person lacks confidence and hope, the act of raising a child can become difficult, even intolerable. This was the situation in San Antonio's Hispanic community until one woman saw the problem and the solution.

It began when Gloria Rodriguez, who holds a doctorate in education, was doing research for her master's degree. She was teaching a group of first-graders who were having problems at school. "At age six they were already destined to fail because they came to school so ill-prepared," Rodriguez says of the children. "I realized that these children were just going to continue having problems unless their parents had the support and the tools they needed to get those children ready for school."

Her imaginative solution was to start a class in the basics of parenting for the mothers of the children. And so Avance—literally *advance* or, in this context, *better yourself*—was born in San Antonio, Texas. Gloria Rodriguez recalls that the idea came to her "almost like a light turning on." Her classic flash of insight was a realization that *being a parent does not come automatically*—that one has to learn the skills, see proper role models, get guidance and support.

When Dr. Rodriguez talked to the children's parents, she found that all of them loved their children and wanted the best for them. They valued education. But she also found out that the children did not come prepared to meet with academic success in the traditional school system. Perhaps most disheartening, virtually all the parents said they expected their children to drop out around seventh or eighth grade, as they themselves had done.

The problem, as Dr. Rodriguez discovered, was that schools often assume that all parents know how to prepare their children for the first years of education. But many of these parents were lacking in the most basic knowledge of how a child grows and develops. Some did not themselves get the proper nurturance when they were children. Others were isolated—they didn't even know their next-door neighbor. They were under continuous stress, and felt hopeless about changing things. About half had symptoms of depression.

Dr. Rodriguez points out that the waves of European immigrants who came to America in this century were met by well-organized resettlement houses, where they were taught the language of their new country, helped with houses and jobs, and shown how the system works. "Unfortunately for too many of us among the Hispanic population," she says, "we did not have that kind of support, and the hope changed to hopelessness, the energy changed to depression. If you provide resources but don't get to that wounded spirit, through love, through encouragement, through positive feedback, the obstacles in their lives will continue to be there. Their own self-perception is their greatest barrier."

The Avance program aims to create a new community. Classes at Avance offer mothers who have been isolated a network of friends and support. Avance staff members are able to say to the other mothers, "I was where you're at and look at me—I've made it and you can, too."

That message is more than inspirational; it has become true for wave after wave of Avance graduates. Starting out on welfare, as dropouts, most go on to get high school equivalency degrees and many get good jobs. One of the main lessons of the program, says Rodriguez, is that "all of us have problems. It's what we do with these problems that makes the difference."

One of the most powerful experiences for many of the mothers in Avance is deceptively simple: a class in toy making. For some mothers, who are so poor that their children have no toys to play with, the chance to make toys for their children is enough to draw them to Avance. One mother explains: "The reason I came to Avance in the first place was toy making. I

ing them. You may be surprised at how this simple effort of giving feedback to get feedback increases your understanding of what is really being said.

GO TO PAGE 169

Mothering at Avance.

wanted toys for my son, but didn't have any money for store-bought ones. When I started in the program, I told myself, I'm not going to pay attention to parenting class. But once I was in the class, I made friends and the lessons were so full of information about my child, about nutrition, all these things."

The toys are designed to speed preschoolers' mastery of basic concepts such as shape and color. For example, one simple toy consists of brightly colored pieces: a square, a triangle, and a circle. In using these shapes to make other objects, such as a doll house, the children begin to recognize the shapes in their own surroundings. And, perhaps as important, the mothers learn how to encourage their children's curiosity instead of squelching it.

Another fundamental lesson for the mothers is in understanding of what is normal, and what is needed, at each stage of a child's development. They see what it means to be their children's first teacher.

The small changes that mothers make in Avance can inspire much larger ones. Perhaps the greatest impact has been on one of the housing projects where many of the Avance mothers live. "It had more than a thousand children," says Dr. Rodriguez, "but there was not one swing in the whole project. And so the mothers said, 'Wait a minute, that's not right. It doesn't have to be this way.' They felt empowered enough to believe they could change things. They told the housing authority: If you want our kids to say no to drugs, to teenage pregnancies, you have to give them some alternatives. And they got $100,000 to build a park." When drug addicts started coming into the neighborhood, the mothers formed a community watch program to take care of one another's homes.

A community is built from small things like making a toy or seeing a child learn. It grows also from seeing their neighbors who attended Avance return to school and find work. All of a sudden people start believing in themselves and what they are capable of doing. And then there's no stopping them.

Through a rare combination of love and practical services, Avance is a catalyst for reducing negative feelings so that these women can move forward with their lives. That is the essence of creative altruism.

"MIGRANT MOTHER": A PHOTOGRAPH STIRS THE NATION

Creative altruism is often spontaneous. An unexpected event, such as the symbiotic meeting of two very different people, can stoke the fires of creativity. Consider what happened to the great American photographer Dorothea Lange.

In March 1936, she had been out on the road for a month, alone. It was late winter, the weather still raw and miserable. It was raining as she drove north for home. Her camera bags were packed.

DOROTHEA LANGE/FPG

Then, out of the corner of her eye, she saw a sign: "PEA-PICKERS CAMP." Something impelled her to stop. "I was following instinct, not reason," she recalled later. "I drove into that wet and soggy camp and parked my car like a homing pigeon. I approached a hungry and desperate mother, as if drawn by a magnet. I do not remember how I explained my presence or my camera to her, but I do remember she asked me no questions."

Lange says, "I did not ask her name or her history. She told me that she was thirty-two. She said that they had been living on frozen vegetables from the surrounding fields and birds that the children killed. She had just sold the tires from her car to buy food.

"There she sat in that lean-to tent with her children huddled around her, and seemed to know that my pictures might help her. And so she helped me. There was a sort of equality about it."

Dorothea Lange could not have known it then, but on this field trip she took one of the great American photographs, "Migrant Mother." Rushed to newspapers all over the country, her picture stirred the consciousness of Americans. It became an important symbol to those who engineered the social programs that finally brought help to the hungry migrants and others suffering in the Depression.

CREATIVE ALTRUISM—
FROM NEPAL TO BRAZIL

BLINDNESS IS one of the many tragic health problems of the Third World. For families living at the poverty line or below, the burden of a blind family member can be extreme. In many poor countries, going blind is virtually a death sentence; the average interval between be coming blind and dying is just three years. Incredibly, more than ninety percent of such blindness is preventable, often through better nutrition for children.

Also, a good deal of blindness is curable. A cataract operation costing fifteen dollars can, in many cases, restore sight. Unfortunately, almost all ophthalmologists are concentrated in major cities, whereas most of the blindness is among villagers scattered through the countryside.

In Nepal, a mountainous country where most people travel by foot, this problem was especially acute. The SEVA Foundation Blindness Project was committed to solving the problem and had mobilized volunteer eye surgeons from Nepal and around the world, but there seemed at first to be no simple way to connect the surgeons with the many blind people in isolated villages.

The solution was to create *eye camps,* mobile surgical teams that travel throughout the countryside. The surgery is often performed in improvised operating rooms, sometimes using school desks as operating tables. But it works. With advance publicity, families know that they can bring their blind relatives to the eye camp for a low-cost operation that will restore the relative's sight on the spot, although it may take several days to walk to the camp.

Creative social action often depends upon perceiving and matching the needs of different groups. The Senior Outreach Program of the Cathedral of St. John the Divine is a clever solution to problems faced by two groups of senior citizens with different needs: physically fit but retired people who are looking for meaningful work, and seniors with physical problems who want to continue living in their own homes instead of in nursing homes.

There are many seniors of both kinds living in the neighborhood surrounding the cathedral. The Senior Outreach Program matches those in their sixties who want and need to be useful, with those, mostly in their late seventies and eighties, who are struggling to maintain their independence. The help given is practical: collecting a Social Security check, filling out medical paperwork, shopping for groceries, or changing a light bulb. Volunteers make daily visits and phone calls to ensure that an elderly person hasn't had a fall or some other mishap.

"It's all part of the idea of hospitality that is central to the fabric of Saint John the Divine," says the cathedral's Paul Gorman. "We take that hospitality to include the older person's right to stay in her home, on her own, as long as possible."

Creative collaboration—the powerful synergy of several different groups—is being used to tackle one of the most dire social problems in our hemisphere. In the 1980s, almost seven million impoverished children lived on the streets of Brazilian cities. With no families, no homes, no school, they roamed in semi-wild bands, getting by as best they could. Little was done for them. Educators labeled the children as dropouts, but despaired of being able to help. Health officials saw them as a public health liability, but felt unable to get them even the most basic services. Businesspeople saw them as a menace, driving away customers by their very presence. The municipal authorities largely turned their backs, and the police eyed the children with suspicion.

The New York–based Synergos Institute, however, came up with a fresh approach. Concerned that no single group could alleviate the problem, Synergos built a partnership among all the groups who could do something for the children. The result was Roda Viva, a collaboration that grew from twenty to four hundred member groups in only a year and a half. The organizers conceived their partnership as a "Living Wheel," where the spokes represent the members joined in equilibrium with each other and with the center, which represents disadvantaged children.

Life for the children gradually started to improve. School buildings

A Nepalese woman recovers from cataract surgery at a SEVA eye camp.

were opened at night so the children could have a place to sleep. Mobile medical clinics were created. Lawyers volunteered to protect the children from harassment and illegal arrest. Sports facilities were provided, and efforts were made to find jobs for the older children. Roda Viva is more than just a solution to a particular problem. With its emphasis on collaboration as a way of addressing deeply rooted problems, it is fast becoming a model for other community partnerships.

NOT JUST BUSINESS AS USUAL

SOME OF OUR most economically successful institutions are also responding to widespread human suffering. Anita Roddick, the businesswoman we met in Chapter Three, believes business is a wonderful medium for altruism "because it's so pragmatic. We look for results."

Her company, the Body Shop, has taken on a series of service projects: helping orphans with AIDS in Romania, fighting the destruction of the rain forest in Brazil, helping the handicapped in communities where the firm has its stores. To encourage personal acts of compassion, employees of the Body Shop are allowed a half day each week of community service, on company time. Employees can choose whatever service they like.

Soon after the communist regime in Romania collapsed, people in the West learned about vast numbers of orphans with AIDS relegated to miserable, grossly understaffed institutions in that country. Roddick explains: "I had been working in Scotland when I saw magazines showing appalling photographs of kids in Romanian orphanages. I wondered what we could do. My daughter was with me, and she suggested organizing something at work. I said fine and when I returned to work, two or three of our staff said to me: can we do something for Romania?

"So we organized a small group of people to run the project and sent a group of what we called the 'guardians' to clean up and paint the whole of three orphanages that had had no aid at all in the north of Moldavia. Then we sent another troupe we called 'the love team' just to hold, love, and look after those babies, most of whom had never been kissed or cuddled."

This may seem a small gesture. But Roddick passionately defends such human-scale efforts. "Why is everybody always obsessed with the big?" she challenges. "What is wrong with that noble one-person interaction, helping that one baby in Romania? People might say that's only a drop in the ocean. So what? If you don't make that drop in the ocean, you won't have that ripple effect." She adds, "I'm not at all interested in changing nations or cultures. I just want to have wonderful examples of the human spirit at play."

One of the most powerful dramas of service to the human spirit is quietly enacted each working day in a factory on the outskirts of Kyoto, Japan. The job prospects of people with severe physical handicaps and mental retardation are usually bleak. Often their suitability for work is judged by whether or not they can perform exactly the same tasks performed by the unimpaired. But Kazuma Tateisi, the founder of Omron, a leading Japanese high-tech company, brought a more humanitarian and creative outlook to the problem. Tateisi took his cue from a branch of engineering science called systems theory, which investigates how parts work together to create a whole that is greater than the sum of the parts. Specifically, he looked at the power of cybernetic engineering to provide an innovative link between the power of humans and the power of machines.

A Japanese assembly line designed to accommodate people in wheelchairs.

His idea was that handicapped persons could work effectively—even on complex assembly lines—if the power of what they were capable of doing was integrated with the power of machines especially designed to utilize their physical strengths. The philosophy is that every person can do something—even if it is only a little something. Omron's Sun House factory features whole assembly lines that have been lowered to the level of wheelchairs. A paralyzed man who can use only one hand uses a tool designed for that hand. A packaging machine is designed to be operated by a woman so severely disabled that she has the energy and mobility for just one slight forward movement. Gently she pushes the carton ahead. With a powerful thrust the machine completes the manufacture of the carton.

In an interdependent world, everything—and *everyone*—should be useful.

Communion of the Sacred and the Secular

O N NEW YORK CITY's Upper West Side, high on a bluff overlooking the heart of Harlem, stands the largest Gothic cathedral in America. Although the construction of the Cathedral of St. John the Divine has been in progress for over a century, it remains incomplete, its stone towers still rising.

Although physically incomplete, the cathedral has become the center of a renaissance in the urban community to whose spiritual needs it ministers. One of those who guides the urban ministry is Dean James Parks Morton. In order to understand how and why this institution is transforming its role today, Dean Morton recalls the role of the cathedral in the equally turbulent times of the Middle Ages. "The medieval cathedral of the later twelfth to fourteenth centuries was a special high-water mark in history," Morton explains. "Cathedrals like Notre Dame and Chartres and Westminster Abbey were built at the same time the first large European cities were coming into being. From the fall of Rome on, there was a decentralized, village civilization in Western Europe. The big cities of the day were in the Orient and the Middle East, not in Europe.

"With the opening up of trade routes, cities formed. That heralded the end of feudalism and the beginning of a new age. And that is when these cathedrals were born. The cathedrals mirrored that new vitality.

"Cities were born, and the cathedrals were born with the cities. In the early days of the Church, cathedrals were very modest in size, perhaps little more than a roof over the chair of the bishop. But with the growth of cities came this new opportunity to symbolize the new ferment.

"The cathedral was a place in which the whole city could gather. These buildings celebrated a unity—that everyone and everything was somehow brought together and lifted up. Government and politics, economics, science and thought, the works of compassion and of art, and, ultimately, the work of worship, all took place in the same space.

"That is why the cathedrals are such great works of art—it was the art of a whole city, of a whole age. And many of the great institutions of the modern world are really children of the cathedrals. The first schools in Western Europe were cathedral schools. And cathedrals were great works of engineering, the greatest of their day, reflecting all kinds of experimentation."

New York, like most great cities, is convulsed with problems. Dean Morton believes that the cathedral should open its doors to this reality. As a result, a good part of the cathedral's budget goes to programs that train and motivate young people.

ROBERT RODRIGUEZ

The towers of the Cathedral of St. John the Divine will be finished sometime next century.

FACING THE STONE

DEAN MORTON points with pride to the stone yard, a vast area to the side of the cathedral where slabs of raw limestone are laboriously chiseled and honed into precisely shaped blocks and artful sculptures that will eventually become part of the cathedral. The stone yard is the site of one of the cathedral's most original experiments aimed at strengthening the life of the community.

For decades, work on the cathedral had stopped. The art of stonecutting was dying. No new generation of apprentices had been trained. Two huge stone towers and several other parts of the cathedral had been abandoned at various stages of completion. When the trustees of the cathedral decided to finish construction, they made a pivotal decision: they would revive the art of stonecutting and create their own stoneyard to be a school for that craft.

For apprentices, the cathedral looked to the neighborhood that stands in its shadows. Many of those who now chisel away at the marble came from families beset by poverty and mired in drug and alcohol dependence.

The stone yard is now world-famous. Stonecutters from the cathe-

A stonecutter at work carving a likeness of Nelson Mandela.

The Creative Spirit

dral have exchanges with their peers in other parts of the world. Stonecutters from France, Russia, and Colombia all share their artistry in this stone yard nestled against one of the great walls of the cathedral.

Many of those who have ended up working in the stone yard are graduates of one of the larger programs of the cathedral, the Manhattan Valley Youth Outreach Program. Up to five thousand young men and women from the surrounding impoverished neighborhoods go through this program each year, whether for the counseling given drug users, pregnant teens or teenage fathers, job training, or any of a half-dozen other services.

Meet Eddie Pizarro, now the boss of the stone yard. "Eddie came from a family in Spanish Harlem with dozens of problems," according to Dean Morton. "But with a lot of sweat and agony, he's succeeded in working his way up from a novice to the head of the stone yard."

"Basically what I do here is try to help somebody else make something of himself," says Pizarro of his work. "I know, because I went through a lot of it, I stumbled a lot. And seeing a lot of guys come through the training makes me feel proud. By teaching a trade, I'm trying to help guys build a life."

For the sixty or so men and women who work in the stone yard, building a life has not been easy. Most come from families and neighborhoods where unemployment, dropping out of school, drug and alcohol abuse, and teen pregnancies are the norm, not the exception. Getting a job of any sort is an accomplishment, let alone mastering a craft.

"What I do here," says Pizarro, "is try to teach them confidence in themselves. A lot of these guys don't know how good they are. This is a lot of hard work, and it takes you a month or two to see that you can really do it. But once you become a craftsman here, you will be able to work all around the world."

The stonecutters in the cathedral have not only revived a dying art, but have earned a reputation for excellence. Their help is sought by urban restorers seeking to rebuild the crumbling stone facades of landmark buildings, and by builders who want stonework for new structures.

Pizarro is justifiably proud of the young people he has brought along. One is Edgar Reyes, a graduate of Manhattan Valley Youth Outreach Pro-

DOES STYROFOAM HAVE AN AFTERLIFE?

Several hundred feet from the main altar of the Cathedral of St. John the Divine there is a very earthy display: a prototype for a rooftop garden. Designed by Paul Mankiewicz and Bill Kinsinger, both with the cathedral's Gaia Institute, it may provide a model for the greening of Manhattan—helping clean the air, cool the city, and provide fresh vegetables.

The prototype offers an innovative but simple solution to a technical problem: how one can create a soil rich enough that it can sustain plant life on a city rooftop, yet light enough that it won't cause the roof to cave in. The idea: use "soil" made partly of shredded polystyrene. Combining the polystyrene with compost creates a light and rich soil. The solution also helps solve another ecological problem: making good use of the dreaded polystyrene found in the billions of styrofoam cups we throw away.

THE ART OF A
CITY IN CONFLICT

The cathedral is also home to an African-American dance company. For Abdel Salaam, leader of the Forces of Nature dance troupe, their performances are part of an urban ministry that aims to foster understanding within the most turbulent neighborhoods of the city.

"The arts have been one of the best ways to help New Yorkers resolve their differences and bring various communities together," Salaam says.

The troupe's repertoire, which features both African and African-American dances, includes a Senegalese dance called "Wolo Sodon Jondon." The dance comes from the

Jon people of Senegal, who were a servant class in the days when many of their people were sold into slavery to be shipped from West Africa to the New World.

"As they saw their brothers and sisters being taken from the country and shipped across the big water," says Salaam, "they saw that their hands and feet were bound. The only thing they could move was their body. And so the dance starts with them moving just their heads and torsos in a slow, dragging movement, because they couldn't move anything else. But in the second part of the dance, the chains break, the feet open up, and the arms become bigger and wilder. This symbolizes the liberation from those things that hold our young people in a state of bondage—poor education, poor housing, disease.

"In the breaking of those chains is a kind of prayer that we are offering our young people, our elders, and the New York community. The prayer is that through the creative spirit inside each of us, we can utilize our vision and free ourselves from conflict."

gram, now a leader in the stone yard. "When Edgar first started, he was the youngest guy here," says Pizarro. "He came from a bad background—he went from foster home to foster home. And when he first came, I used to take him home with me and tell him, Listen, you've got to try to learn everything you can. Someday, I told him, you'll be good at it. And you will be somebody. Today Edgar is my right-hand man."

In the course of developing craft skills, many apprentices come face to face with ingrained habits and self-defeating attitudes. Pizarro says, "I'm hoping that they learn not only about stonecutting, but about life: how to achieve a goal. It is pretty rough for a lot of these neighborhood guys because a lot of them don't know what they really could do if they tried. They quit, they say, 'I can't do that.' It's up to guys like me to bring out of them what they can really do.

"Attitude has a lot to do with it. A lot of people who come from the streets have the attitude that life is just about surviving. They don't see that you can do more than just survive.

"Four years in an apprenticeship is hard. Some people can't even hold a marriage together that long. It's a big sacrifice, four years going to school, learning the trade. The hardest part is getting themselves to get up in the morning and come over here and face the stone. But one of the best feelings you have here is to cut a stone and actually see it placed up in the cathedral. And for somebody else to see it and say, Wow, look at all the hard work someone has put into that."

Reyes reflects: "It takes a long time to build a cathedral. I know I may not see the finish of it. Hopefully, my children will. The cathedral is being built by people for their own community. I can say, 'I built that.' I can show people: this is what I did."

Despite these dramatic success stories, Dean Morton is often asked why a cathedral so dedicated to practical community action is expending resources on completing a stone tower. In response, he tells an ancient Buddhist tale of a beggar who has two coins: With one he buys bread. With the other he buys an exquisite flower.

"We are more than just our stomachs," says Morton. "Our spirits have to be fed, too. And the tower, which is a beautiful thing, symbolizes

I Am a Camera

HERE'S AN exercise you can do with a friend. It can be enjoyable and give you an experience of seeing without preconceptions.

℮ Decide which person will be the camera and who will be the photographer. If you play the camera, your friend as the photographer should stand behind you. Assume that your eyes are the camera lens and your right shoulder is the shutter button. Your eyes (the lens) are to be shut until the photographer takes a photograph by tapping you on the right shoulder (pressing the shutter). At that instant your eyes open and close quickly, just as the shutter of a camera does.

The role of the photographer is to walk you around, guiding you by your shoulders and positioning you so that different scenes will be in your line of vision. The photographer then "takes a picture" by depressing the shutter button (tapping your right shoulder). The photographer should take care not to bump or break the camera, of course. Assume there are twelve to twenty-four frames on this roll of film, so keep moving and snapping (tapping).

Your task, as camera, is to record every detail of the picture perfectly, with no distortion. Trust that the photographer knows what he or she is doing. When the shutter button is pressed, the your eyes open for only a brief moment—just a second will do—and the image in view is recorded on the film (in your memory). All you have to do is to see what's there in front of you, *without any preconceived notions* for each of the pictures you take. ℮

There are a couple of reasons to do this. The rapid series of recorded impressions gives you the experience of seeing what is, without perception being filtered through your expectations. It's the seeing without any predetermined concepts that's important. As many inventors, such as Paul MacCready (see page 36), will tell you, reducing your preconceptions when you face a new problem is a vital element in the creative process.

GO TO PAGE 172

in a very real way the community that is building it. And the people who built it can say, 'My grandson is going to be working on that.' And my grandson is going to say, 'My grandfather built that.' That's wonderful."

✳◎✳
A SYMBIOTIC COMMUNITY

THERE IS A FASCINATING MIX of the secular and the sacred at the cathedral. Dean Morton believes that this was also the case in the Middle Ages. "One of my pet stories," says Morton, "is of the great cathedral at Chartres, which was built on the town square so that the market was right outside its doors. Many people take as a mark of piety of the cathedral's builders the fact that the floor inclines as you go toward the altar, as if you are rising to heaven.

"I say that's nonsense. It's right on the marketplace, and when it rained I'm sure everything in the market went inside—all the chickens and pigs and everything else. I think it slopes because they had to hose it down afterward. That's one of my favorite images of the sacred and secular being fused. And that is what we are trying to bring about again—that natural blending of this place and the community."

For Dean Morton, the very diversity of the community is the source of its creativity. Differences allow for *symbiosis,* the beneficial relationship between two dissimilar beings. That is both a scientific and a religious concept. Creative altruism comes out of community. The community—if it is alive— is, like the cathedral, always a work in progress. Like life itself, the community is constantly evolving, making mistakes, foundering, and then forging ahead. This evolution is the product of both creativity and compassion.

It is the best of times, and the worst of times. A time to rethink the nature of our responsibility for others and to expand the limits of our caring. Acts of creative altruism place us at the center of the web of life, drawing us into an intimate relationship with others. One hope is that the peoples of the world will grow stronger from this inevitable coming together and that a vigorous new global culture will arise from diversity. But what would be the conditions for such a renaissance of human creativity?

Igniting a Global Renaissance of Creativity

THROUGHOUT HISTORY there have been times and places where people have been especially inventive and creative. Scholars tell us that such periods have been spurred by an abundance of differing viewpoints, a welcome environment for change, and a driving necessity to solve problems. For example, in the United States, a brute fact of history may have made America particularly receptive to the creative spirit.

In the view of Howard Gardner, the problems faced on the American frontier demanded a creative response: "So often the inventiveness came out of a real practical problem on the frontier, on the farm, in the wilderness, where there were no precedents, no how-to books, no handy wise people to go to for guidance," Gardner observes. "People, young and old, had to put their heads together until they arrived at a solution."

The conditions for a creative renaissance have been explored by Dean Simonton's research at the University of California. His conclusion is that throughout history, intense rivalries among small states have often sparked creativity. Ancient Greece, home to some of the world's most original thinkers, was divided into numerous city-states, like Corinth, Athens, and Sparta. Likewise, the Italy of the Renaissance was bubbling with political intrigue between rival city-states like Florence and Venice, each a brewing pot for its own form of creativity from which emerged the likes of Michelangelo, Raphael, Dante, Machiavelli, and Leonardo. And it was during the centuries when what is now Germany comprised a mosaic of small principalities, that Mozart, Beethoven, Goethe, Hegel, and Schiller offered their ge-

Penetrating Questions

DURING PERIODS of great change, answers don't last very long but a question is worth a lot. The word *question* is derived from the Latin *quaerere* (to seek), which is the same root as the word for *quest*. A creative life is a continued quest, and good questions are useful guides. We have found that the most useful questions are open-ended; they allow a fresh, unanticipated answer to reveal itself.

These are the kind of questions children aren't afraid to ask. They seem naive at first. But think how different our lives would be if certain questions of wonder were never asked. Jim Collins of Stanford's Graduate School of Business has compiled the following list of questions of wonder:

Albert Einstein: What would a light wave look like to someone keeping pace with it?

Bill Bowerman (inventor of Nike shoes): What happens if I pour rubber into my waffle iron?

Fred Smith (founder of Federal Express): Why can't there be reliable overnight mail service?

Godfrey Hounsfield (inventor of the CAT scanner): Why can't we see in three dimensions what is inside a human body without cutting it open?

Masaru Ibuka (honorary chairman, Sony): Why don't we remove the re-

nius to the world. When Bismarck unified Germany in the late nineteenth century, however, the German Golden Age drew to a close. As Gladstone put it: "He made Germany great and Germans small."

These are not just isolated examples; this pattern runs deep in the currents of history. That is Simonton's conclusion from an ambitious study measuring the number of outstanding creators between 500 B.C. and A.D. 1899 throughout the great civilizations of Europe, India, China, and the Islamic world. He found that wealth, geographic growth, a centralized nation, and warfare all failed to show any relationship to creativity. The one factor that was linked to a creative spurt was political fragmentation.

Simonton then scrutinized 127 twenty-year periods in European history, from 700 B.C. to A.D. 1839. Again, political fragmentation emerged as the single best political predictor of creativity. Creative development, to some extent, depends on exposure to cultural diversity.

The most recent Golden Age of creativity in America peaked after World War II. "We began to be highly creative in all domains, becoming world leaders," says Simonton. "Most of the world looked to us for leadership in all the various fields of science, of art, of the humanities in general." One reason for this creative spurt, Simonton notes, was America's ability to draw upon the diversity of its own people, whether refugees from Europe or African-Americans.

⊚

CITIZENS OF THE MONOLITH, REBEL!

INDEED, A CHILDHOOD spent amid a profusion of cultural differences and contrary viewpoints is a tonic for the creative spirit. Most eminent philosophers, for instance, grew up in a time and place marked by political fragmentation. Professor Simonton has found that there was roughly a twenty-year lag time in the flowering of creativity. Small rival states instilled a creative attitude in their children, which came to fruition when they reached adulthood—even when the nation itself underwent an overall unification and conformity. "Aristotle was the teacher of Alexander the

Great," says Simonton, "but tiny Athens and not the Macedonian Empire must take credit for Aristotle's intellectual development." The creative course for those born a citizen of a monolithic state: rebel! Most of the great philosophers espoused a credo that ran contrary to the norms of the time.

Competitive entrepreneurial companies today are not unlike the rival city-states of the past. As the natural history of corporations has shown time and again, when an entrepeneurial company succeeds beyond all expectations, growing practically overnight into a huge business, then the creative spark is in danger of extinction, just as happens in monolithic states. "Large institutions stifle change," says Stanford University's Jim Collins. "Why is it that the Western economies were so much more innovative than the old massive, centralized East bloc economies? Because you have far more room for creativity when you keep things small than you do in one giant economic monolith."

Simonton notes interesting parallels between individual and societal creativity. At the individual level, creativity involves a process of taking in new ideas, of being thrown into a disequilibrium and trying to reach some accommodation, achieve a new synthesis. The creative process involves integrating the parts into some coherent whole. But to remain creative the individual has to keep assimilating new information and new experiences.

The same is true at the societal level. In the most creative periods there has been a tremendous infusion of diversity: new ideas and cross-cultural encounters. Then the society is confronted with putting all this diversity and complexity together in some harmonious way. In the best of all possible worlds, that society becomes creative and enters a golden age in which it manages to parlay its diversity into a unique style or vision of the world.

Simonton believes that America may be poised to experience a new burst of creativity. He points to the existence of major populations of African and of Hispanic origin and a huge infusion of immigrants from the Pacific Rim and Southeast Asia. This diversity now exists in small, splintered communities, but if we can find some way to draw the strength of this plurality into a unified vision, Simonton feels that America can continue to be one of the most creative nations in the world.

cording function and speaker and put headphones in the recorder? (Result: the Sony Walkman.)

Many of these questions were deemed ridiculous at first. Other shoe companies thought Bowerman's waffle shoe was a "really stupid idea." Godfrey Hounsfield was told the CAT scan was "impractical." Masaru Ibuka got comments like: "A recorder with no speaker and no recorder—are you crazy?" Fred Smith proposed the idea of Federal Express in a paper at Yale and got a C.

Here's a simple exercise you can do to develop your ability to ask questions that can produce radically new and unexpected ideas. Each day, for a week, take a few minutes to ask yourself a question that begins: "I wonder....." Ask this question about a particular area of your life, such as the workplace. "I wonder what would happen if we divided the corporation into twelve, smaller, autonomous companies?" It is essential not to censor yourself, no matter how impractical or outlandish the question sounds.

After you have had some practice doing this, try going public with your questions by posing them to friends or colleagues. Focus on something you are sincerely curious about and that matters to others. Listen carefully to their responses. As in the story of the Emperor's New Clothes, you'll probably discover that your question reveals blind spots and assumptions that deserve to be challenged.

In Europe, major ethnic groups who have been dominated for decades by huge empires are now using their new freedom to look back into their past and say, What is unique about being a Slav or a Pole? The homogeneity that was artificially imposed over Eastern Europe and the Soviet Union has now been lifted, and in its place will grow nerve centers of creativity.

Further, because of global communication, there is more opportunity than ever for cultures to learn from one another. Cultures weak in one or another area of creativity can learn from another society strong in that area, as Japan has successfully done in adopting Western technology.

Ultimately, a renaissance in creativity will depend upon the actions of individuals. A Swedish worker proudly stamps his name on the part of the machine he has made. A Detroit neurosurgeon tenderly places her hand on the head of her infant patient and searches for special clues to a more successful operation. An Italian child looks wide-eyed at the dazzling beauty of a field of poppies and announces that it's "better than ice cream." But the last words on the subject of creativity must go to a woman who was blind and deaf.

Helen Keller remembered talking to a friend who had just returned from a long walk in the woods. When she asked her friend what she had observed, her friend replied, "Nothing in particular."

"I wondered how it was possible," Helen said, "to walk for an hour through the woods and see nothing of note. I who cannot see find hundreds of things: the delicate symmetry of a leaf, the smooth skin of a silver birch, the rough, shaggy bark of a pine. I who am blind can give one hint to those who see: use your eyes as if tomorrow you will have been stricken blind.

"Hear the music of voices, the song of a bird, the mighty strains of an orchestra as if you would be stricken deaf tomorrow.

"Touch each object as if tomorrow your tactile sense would fail.

"Smell the perfume of flowers, taste with relish each morsel, as if tomorrow you could never taste or smell again.

"Make the most of every sense.

"Glory in all the facets and pleasures and beauty which the world reveals to you."

"If one advances in the direction of his dreams, one will meet with success unexpected in common hours."
—HENRY DAVID THOREAU

© Warner Bros. Inc. 1988

We would like to thank the following individuals who helped produce "The Creative Spirit" television series:

SENIOR PRODUCER & WRITER
Paul Kaufman

SERIES PRODUCER & DIRECTOR
Catherine Tatge

PRODUCERS
Lisa Sonne
Sunde Smith

ANIMATION AND
GRAPHICS PRODUCER
John Andrews

ASSOCIATE PRODUCERS
Anne-Marie B. Cunniffe
Anne Hansen

DIRECTORS OF PHOTOGRAPHY
Joel Shapiro
Nancy Schreiber

MUSIC COMPOSED
AND CONDUCTED BY
Benny Golson

VIDEOTAPE EDITORS
Girish Bhargava
Lisa Jackson

SERIES ANIMATION AND TITLES
John Canemaker

"CREATIVITY TIPS"
"CREATIVITY KILLERS"
"THE BOSS"
Snowden/Fine Productions

NEWS ANIMATIONS
Fabrika

PAINTBOX GRAPHICS
Ada Whitney
Steve Sullivan
Sharon Haskell

ADDITIONAL ARTWORK
Deborah Dawson

POST-PRODUCTION
Telstar Editing

SUPERVISING EDITOR
Girish Bhargava

ON-LINE EDITOR
Bill Stephan

EFFECTS EDITING
Paul Srp

ASSISTANT EDITORS
Laura Young
Andrea Gurwitt

SOUND MIXING
Grant Maxwell
Sync Sound, Inc.

MUSIC RECORDING
Gary Chester
National Recording Studios, Inc.

POST-PRODUCTION COORDINATOR
Elizabeth Soriano

PRODUCTION MANAGER
Susan Levinson Bixby

SERIES DEVELOPED BY
Lisa Sonne

PRODUCTION ASSISTANTS
Ellen Egeth
Terence Williams

ADDITIONAL PHOTOGRAPHY
Mark W. Chamberlin
Marc Kroll
Jeorg Walters

AUDIO/VIDEO
Eddie O'Connor

GRIP/ELECTRICIANS
Kelly James Richardson
Hiroyuki Morita
Hajime Toda
Sung Y. Pak

MUSICIANS
Benny Golson
Bill Mays
Ray Drummond
Marvin Smith
Art Farmer
Robbie Kondor
John Moses
Frank Morelli
Karen Griffin
Stephen Taylor

MUSIC CONTRACTOR
Emile Charlap

PROJECT ADMINISTRATION
Nancy Pelz-Paget
Rick Porter
John Lestarchick
Jane Schulberg
Elizabeth Benson
Karin Huntzinger
Elizabeth Martin

SERIES CREATED BY
Paul Kaufman

COORDINATING PRODUCER
Douglas P. Sinsel

EXECUTIVE PRODUCER
Alvin H. Perlmutter

The Creative Spirit was a production of Alvin H. Perlmutter, Inc. The series was made possible by a grant from IBM.

Index

About the Authors

DANIEL GOLEMAN is a psychologist who covers the behavioral sciences for the *New York Times*. His articles from the *Times* are syndicated throughout the English-speaking world. He was for many years a senior editor at *Psychology Today*, and he has taught psychology at Harvard University. He is also the author of seven books, among them *Vital Lies, Simple Truths* and *The Meditative Mind*. He has received numerous awards for his writing, including a Lifetime Achievement Award from the American Psychological Association.

PAUL KAUFMAN is the creator, writer, and senior producer of "The Creative Spirit" television series. A veteran documentary filmmaker, he recently produced and wrote "The Truth about Lies," part of the 1989 Peabody Award-winning series "The Public Mind." He has also explored the subject of creativity as Visiting Research Associate at Harvard University's Carpenter Center for the Visual Arts, where he investigated the nature of visual thinking and the use of images to express concepts, and as Senior Research Associate at Stanford University, where he conducted research into the importance of values in the interpretation of information.

MICHAEL RAY holds the McCoy-Banc One chair of Creativity and Innovation at Stanford University's Graduate School of Business. His work and courses have received international attention in both print and broadcast media for their innovative approaches to creativity in business and everyday life. He is the co-author of three books, *The Path of the Everyday Hero*, *Creativity in Business*, and *New Traditions in Business*, as well as a recipient of the World Business Academy's Harman Award.